*For my mother
who must have taught me
how to laugh.*

Malice in Blunderland

or How the Grits Stole Christmas

Peterson

Allan Fotheringham

Malice in Blunderland
or How the Grits Stole Christmas

Key Porter Books

Canadian Cataloguing in Publication Data

Fotheringham, Allan, 1932-
    Malice in Blunderland, or, How the grits stole
Christmas
ISBN 0-919493-01-7
1. Canada — Politics and government — 1968-1979 —
Anecdotes, facetiae, satire, etc.* 2. Canada —
Politics and government — 1979-1980 — Anecdotes,
facetiae, satire, etc.* 3. Canada — Politics and
government — 1980-   — Anecdotes, facetiae,
satire, etc.* I. Title. II. Title: How the grits
stole Christmas.
FC630.F68   971.064'4'0207   C82-095124-2
F1034.2.F68

Key Porter Books
59 Front Street East
Toronto M5E 1B3

Designed by David Shaw
Printed and bound in Canada
by T. H. Best Printing Company Limited

Contents

Introduction / 9

1 The Maritimes: Down to the Sea in Rigs / 15
2 Quebec: Divorce with Bed Privileges / 31
3 First Stopover: The Sidewalks of Montreal / 43
4 First Digression: Trudeau's Cabinet / 51
5 Second Stopover: Ottawa Revisited with a Vengeance /
6 Second Digression: The Bachelor Party / 81
7 Ontario: The Complacency Capital of the World / 87
8 Third Stopover: Toronto, the Big Lemon / 95
9 Third Digression: Confessions of a
      Closet Enthusiast / 109
10 Manitoba: The Fun Beneath the Surface / 115
11 Saskatchewan: The Unconscious Force / 131
12 Fourth Digression: Notwithstanding Lawyers / 147
13 Alberta: Man-Boys in the Promised Land / 153
14 British Columbia: Narcissus-on-the-Pacific / 171
15 Fourth Stopover: The Village on the Edge
      of the Rain Forest / 187
16 Fifth Digression: The Pretenders / 201
17 Finale: Trudeau Today is Nowhere at All / 209

Acknowledgements / 223

Introduction

Someone, God knows, has to save the country. There are those of us who feel so sympathetic to Ottawa — home of all that is good, dedicated and smarmy — that we refuse to reside there. We prefer the perspective of the starship, otherwise known as the People's Republic Airline, home of the toy meals and the geriatric stewardae: Air Canada. Those of us who prefer to view Canada from seven miles high, rather than deal with its depressing reality at street level, spend our fitful lives at luggage carousels, waiting for the mangled remains of our underwear.

The peripatetic life, while ravaging to the liver, the mind and the suitcase, does have one beneficial aspect: it is the view of the *thread*. If one puts down in enough airports, bunks in enough plastic hotel rooms, wrestles often enough with Air Canada cutlery that must have been designed by a vegetarian on a fast, certain patterns become apparent. The skeleton of the land that is not strong becomes clear.

The thread that unites the country is the distaste for the Natural Governing Party, alias the Liberals. Their major mistake, as it turns out, was to snatch that Pyrrhic victory from the boy amateurs of Joe Why on that infamous 1979 budget night. It prevented the Liberals from cleansing their souls, renovating their machinery and scrubbing their leader.

Thrust back in power by the incompetence of a nervous Tory prime minister who shot himself in the foot after only seven months, the Liberals discovered they had nothing left in the holster themselves.

Wherever the plane lands, wherever the stomach groans and cries for live food, one finds the same vibrations: these Grits are men (and the occasional woman) who are out of synch with the country. They are not evil, but incompetent. Not corrupt, but bankrupt of ideas. Their arrogance is supreme, their smugness sublime, their ignorance of reality bottomless.

The starship cruises overhead; the traveller gazing down in bewilderment at this collection of brains, led by the finest intellect of our age, a man now cosmically removed from real life, who heads a cabinet that was so eager to regain power for power's sake that it neglected to find any real reason for doing so.

The prisoner in the starship, issuing little yelps of disbelief at what he sees, cruises on.

What follows is a disconnected overview from thirty-five thousand feet of the present political situation. It is not a neat package, but neither is Canada in 1982, thanks to the Grits.

The digressions from slavish theme are purposeful, the wandering thoughts of a reporter who makes a living by bouncing down at airports, snatching insights and gossip and bounding off again, destined for the next deadline. Canada is the second largest country in the world (filled entirely with jealousy). This is not the perfect way to fathom it, but it is preferable, one submits, to sitting in Ottawa in the belief that the capital is relevant to the populace.

It isn't. Its insularity is apparent to all but those who live there and rule from there. It's a sad town, in that it lives on the illusion that it is in touch. Ottawa is the civic equivalent of the man in the insane asylum who contents himself in the belief that he is Napoleon. It needs its head tapped, but those in charge are victims of the same disorder.

What Constant Reader will find here are the author's random inanities on the state of our peril. Some faint traces

10

of outraged thought may be recognized from previous angry periods in both newspaper and magazine scribblings, but no one should be alarmed. Some exquisite assessments are too precious to throw away, some memorable paeans to particular cabinet ministers deserve a second glance. A Reggie Jackson swing, while striking out, deserves to be captured by instant replay and contemplated again.

Landings in Manitoba inspire thoughts pertaining to the permutations in the prime minister's personal entourage; pitstops in Prince Edward Island recall happenings in Nanton, Alberta. The country is connected only by those who flit about it, trailing spider webs of rumour behind them. The journalist's mind is not a solid academic lump; it is stitched together by interconnections, wild leaps and stale anecdotes. The man in the starship is as a stone skipping across the water, making little impact, but touching down often, too often.

These views of the Grits at play have been gathering during fourteen years of writing columns, an indenture coinciding with the term of the Trudeau career as prime minister. They are written, in this summer of 1982, in the belief that a prime minister who went to Ottawa to save one portion of the country has almost succeeded in driving away another section of it.

The views will demonstrate the prejudices and background of a Western Canadian who now lives half the year in Ottawa in an attempt to educate it. I maintain two residences, one in Vancouver and the other in Ottawa, shuttling between them because, as mentioned, God knows someone has to save the country. Those at the top certainly aren't doing it.

If, in the line of duty, I did not persist in the crazy experiment of living in Ottawa two weeks in every month, I would be forced to live there for four weeks a month — something that no sane, civilized man would do. A chap has to nibble at the apple to discover the worm at the core.

Living in two cities does not, as Constant Reader might assume, lead to a permanent state of jet-lag. The human body is remarkably adaptable to most things, save perhaps the verbiage of Allan MacEachen, and becomes accustomed to four-hour-and-forty-five-minute transitions through the Alley Oop 747 time machine.

Although I hate airplanes, air terminals, air dogfood, airline computers and luggage merry-go-rounds, I like being in the air. (The only thing that spoils it is that airlines are in charge of it.) It is the one chance in life, aside from death, when one is spared telephones, ladies from the Red Feather Drive, traffic, and people who want to know in what round Jack Dempsey knocked out Louis Firpo, the Wild Bull of the Pampas.

The journalist is the most interrupted person on earth, everyone assuming that anyone who can solve the daily problems of the globe in one Olympian eight-hundred word chomp does not mind having his tenuous train of thought flagged down at every second paragraph. Only on a plane can one have four hours and forty-five minutes of uninterruption. The best thing about the silver cigar is that it is, usually, packed with complete strangers. One is enveloped in a cocoon of formality; Canadians being as emotionally constricted as they fortunately are, no one is eager to plunge into conversational foreplay if discouraged by a lofty visage. The ordinary earthbound Canadian cannot buy, with whatever money, a week that includes four hours and forty-five minutes of selfish, soulful time to read and ruminate.

The greatest aid to this stealing of silence is the Sony Walkman, which one attaches to one's ears — with the sound off — while gazing out at the limpid ozone over Thunder Bay. When the seatmate ventures some witticism, one only shakes one's head, as if a deaf mute, seemingly oblivious. The disguise works. You can even shake off the dogfood.

To save the country, all that is required is two homes, two cars, two wardrobes and two sets of tennis gear. If anyone would question my devotion to the nation, he need only judge the patriotism required in owning two Prince racquets.

The one insoluble problem is my books. I cannot really clone my library. Dividing them in half, by flipping a coin, doesn't work. Invariably, when the scribbler at 1 AM in Vancouver wants to look up a reference detailing Eugene Whelan's charisma quotient, the book is in Ottawa. And vice versa. The country's salvation may have to await a personal data bank.

Instead of jet-lag, I am twice monthly injected with a most useful syringe of culture shock, the medicine that keeps me so mellow and tolerant, not to mention wise. Flying from the bureaucratic beehive of Ottawa to The Village on the Edge of the Rain Forest is travelling from the edge of night to the edge of the abyss.

Another result of my continually flitting from the ridiculous to the sublime is that Air Canada usually shows a profit in its yearly statements. Take Dr. Foth from its accounts and it is reduced to the revenues of Air Liberia. I will be crushed if my suitcase is not eventually bronzed and mounted in the People's Republic Airline boardroom, alongside the Plasticine bust of Bryce Mackasey.

The qualifications for dispensing the upcoming wisdom are clear. I have now followed Pierre Trudeau and his forelock-tugging forelock-tuggers through five elections. I have chased him through Italy, London, Sweden, Norway and the mental obbligatos of at least four press secretaries. It may not have been quite as much fun as it was going around the world in 80 daze with Joe Clark and his wandering luggage, but it has been useful.

At one stage, I attempted to drive from Halifax to Vancouver, to tap the intellect of every truck-stop waitress and gas jockey in Canada as to the true gut feeling of the populace. About a third of the way through the kidney-jarring expedition, the 1979 election was called and while I interrogated the pizza parlour bus boys of the nation, my mates in the Press Gallery zoomed overhead at thirty-five thousand feet. The starship had become earthbound. (The food on the ground was better.)

Eventually, I abandoned the insane idea at Edmonton and rejoined the political jet-set. Nothing had changed. The press secretaries were still handing out the mandatory

"Gainesburgers" — chow to fill the wire services and the thirty-second radio clips — after the regular champagne-and-orange-juice that started each morning's flight.

I toughed it out because I long ago determined that God in Her wisdom placed me on this planet so as to keep the Liberals humble. It's a nasty job, but somebody has to do it.

Those who huddle in the thumb-sucking comfort of Ottawa are automatically disqualified from assessing the Natural Governing Party. The Liberals own the town, and everyone who makes a buck there knows it and must feed off that fact. Only those who owe their allegiance to the boondocks have the perspective, through the wrong end of the telescope, to see the Grits as they are.

This is a view through the wrong end of the telescope. It is a fix on a party from afar. It is sympathetic, charitable — and exactly what they deserve.

1
The Maritimes
Down to the Sea in Rigs

Peckford's bad boy . . .
offshore wrongs . . . the DREE spree, or,
boondoggle in the boondocks . . .
the movable Hatfield . . . the immovable Camp . . .
poor MacEachen

Newfoundland

This journey through the minds of the Trudeaucrats, this incursion into the craniums of those who would steal our patrimony, begins in Newfoundland. It is the home of Liberal icons Joey Smallwood and Don Jamieson — and John Crosbie, once a Liberal, now a Tory, the only man in the House of Commons who doesn't speak either of the two official languages. The fourteen years of Pierre Trudeau hegemony have destroyed Newfie's Grit link: Premier Brian Peckford's April 1982 election returned an astonishing forty-four Conservatives to the legislature of an island brought into Canada by a bow-tied Liberal who is the only living Father of Confederation.

Joey Smallwood, having mother-henned the narrow 1948 Confederation vote, inveigled the gentle Lester Pearson into a prime ministerial open-convertible parade through downtown St. John's. The opening cars of the cavalcade were blocked in traffic causing the Smallwood-Pearson car to come to halt outside a pub, where a bleary citizen shook his fist at the trapped Liberal dignitaries and gave them the benefit of his asterisked eloquence. As a pink-faced Pearson squirmed in discomfort, Joey turned to him and calmly announced, "I think we'll have to put him down as 'undecided.'" Today, there are few Canadians who are undecided about how the once lordly Liberals under Trudeau have dismembered the country.

On that day in 1948 when Newfoundland narrowly decided to join Canada, millionaire's son John Crosbie and his brother Andrew, along with future Newfoundland premier Frank Moores, stood on the dining room table of the exclusive St. Andrew's private school outside Toronto. The Crosbie boys, sent to a Central Canada polishing school, had blacked their faces with shoe polish. The black laces of their rugby boots hung from them in mourning, and with tears streaming down their faces, they sang "I'll Always Be A Newfoundlander."

Perhaps, but not always a Liberal. Crosbie, the Tory, now sits in the Commons, a strangely suspended figure, watching the Liberals, who mocked his 1979 budget and defeated his government on it, flounder on budgets that resemble Swiss cheese. Allan J. MacEachen (Allan J. Ferragamo to insiders) — who devised the Tory downfall — has screwed up far more than Finance Minister John Crosbie ever did, but he does it with unction, a quality unknown to Crosbie, his fellow Maritimer. That Canada should have successive finance ministers from the most impoverished region of the Dominion may help explain why we are in our present pickle.

Newfoundland is a rock covered with three inches of dirt. Entire grown forests look as if they had been stricken with rickets, resembling thousand-year-old Japanese dwarf trees. Newfie joke: how many Liberals does it take to make chocolate-chip cookies? Six. Two to bake and four to peel the Smarties. Crosbie, a gold medallist at law school who talks like a barroom brawler, has done more to make the Newf patois lovable than anything, including The Mummers. Speaking of loyalty to Joe Clark, he told the Commons: "We stand back to back, cheek to cheek, belly to belly, bum to bum."

The only person who doesn't think he's funny is Joe Clark. But Clark never laughs, at least not in public, which is wise because it makes him sound as if he has been injected with teen-age senility.

Thanks to modern technology, Newfoundlanders no longer

lose their sons in fishboats. They lose them in "unsinkable" offshore oil rigs. "If it floats," said an old St. John's fisherman after the *Ocean Ranger* went down, "it can sink."

So can Liberal common sense. With eighty-four dead, most of them Canadians, most of them Newfoundlanders, Ottawa engaged in a struggle with the province as to who would hold the official inquiry into the tragedy. Within weeks, Canadians were treated to the sight of the swift Americans holding their own inquiry, since the rig was U.S. owned. Parents of dead Canadian boys who were drilling for Canadian oil in Canadian waters had to get their first facts on the *Ocean Ranger*'s sinking from hearings in Boston and New Orleans. Bobby Kennedy, bitter over Ottawa's dithering in a Washington crisis, once said, "In an emergency, Canada will offer you all aid short of help." The mothers of the *Ocean Ranger* dead now know the feeling.

The dispute over dead men, so insane from the outside, is at the base of Newfoundland's quarrel with Ottawa. The real struggle is over which government has jurisdiction over the mineral resources offshore. Whoever got to hold the *Ocean Ranger* inquiry might claim it established a precedent. While the two sides in the ghoulish squabble finally agreed on a joint inquiry, we got our basic facts from the speedy Americans.

So wonderful have the relations between the Trudeaucrats and the proud Newfoundlanders become that the two governments refuse to get into the same room together when they exchange money. In February, Transport Minister Jean-Luc Pépin travelled to St. John's to put his signature on a federal-provincial transportation document. It committed the feds to providing seventy-five percent of planned expenditures of some $70 million — mainly for highways and ferry terminals.

After fifteen months of negotiation, much of it acrimonious in the great Canadian tradition, Premier Brian Peckford sat in his office in the Confederation Building, home of the Newfoundland legislature. Pépin sat in the Hotel Newfoundland miles away in downtown St. John's, insisting it was a "convention" that transportation agreements are signed at that hotel. Neither would budge.

So Pépin signed his little piece of paper and forty-five minutes later, Peckford signed it. Two children in their tree forts, sticking their tongues out at each other. So marches the progress of Ottawa's relations with its provinces.

Premier Peckford is an English teacher with the temperament of a four-year-old. He inherited that classic Newfoundland tetchiness toward the condescension of the lords on high from Ottawa, which Pierre Absolutely Trendy carries around with him like after-shave lotion. The prime minister is like catnip to provincial premiers: his arrogance is the best thing they've got going at the polls. If they were smart, they'd send him a cheque in a plain brown wrapper.

The party that brought Newfoundland into Canada is now shut out, seen as a stiff-necked protector of central power. The man's gifts of alienation are marvellous to behold, somewhat like his trampoline backflips.

It seems a peculiar way to run a country in that the prime minister, by insisting on a disputatious style with the ten premiers he clearly regards as inferiors, ensures their popularity at home. It is said that Harold Ballard as a child was so unpleasant they had to tie pork chops around his neck so at least the dog would play with him. Pierre Trudeau displays the same flair for federal-provincial relations.

The best method theatre at the fed-prov confabs, right out of Lee Strasberg, is the eyeball-to-eyeball between new boy Peckford and the man at the head of the horseshoe table.

As luck would have it — seniority actually, as the seating is arranged on the order of entry into Confederation — directly opposite Trudeau, at the other end of the gun barrels of his steely gaze, sits Peckford with the TV cameras boring into the bristles on the back of his neck.

Peckford is shirty, prickly, with eyes that dart like dark cherries plugged into an electric guitar. He epitomizes, in his nervous body language, all the resentments that a new generation of educated Newfies store in their gut against the colonial masters from Ottawa. Newfoundland, as the newcomer among provinces, has yet to get out of her system the feeling that she is regarded as a babe among adults.

Peckford, sparks shooting off him, cannot wait to get his gums into the microphone but must fidget while the familiar litany from the other premiers with seniority is spilled into the maw of the Holy Mother Corporation's cameras.

Trudeau sits at the top of the horseshoe, his eyes glinted into that familiar Egyptian mask configuration, attempting to zap the interloper with ESP electrodes. He is the supreme actor of our time, never more aloof in his role than when the cameras are on him. This is why Clark, by comparison, is such an uncomfortable television figure, his nervous mannerisms too obvious, the fake pomposity that is designed to hide them even more apparent. Trudeau is just as stagey as Clark; the difference is that he is a superb actor. Clark is a lousy one.

Peckford is the adventuresome pup, making tentative darts at Trudeau, the sly old cat who sits, never twitching, oblivious, only occasionally with exquisite timing reaching out to swat the inexperienced intruder. All that's needed is a fireplace and the image of the tabby teaching the pup lessons he will never forget is complete.

The prime minister, in the arch manner that used to so endear him to the farmer premier of P.E.I., Angus MacLean, trots out a favourite quote learned at the Sorbonne, or perhaps the London School of Economics. The former English teacher Peckford, feeling it an aimed insult, snaps back an apt quotation from the reservoir of his memory.

The others who have seen this movie before, Lougheed, the now-departed Blakeney and the wily Davis, smile quietly to themselves and watch the pup lunge at the tabby before the fireplace.

Nova Scotia

Nova Scotia is the refuge of George Bain, the wittiest columnist ever to grace Ottawa, and the Toronto-loving Harry Bruce, who finally decided that a swimming pool in the shape of his ulcer was not his dominant goal in life and retreated to the province that is known as Canada's home for the emotionally tired.

Bruce moved through the media maze in Toronto in successful stints in magazines and newspapers before deciding that Halifax was the last stop. Confounding all the predictions of doom, he was the founding editor of *Atlantic Insight*, a beautifully produced magazine that has walked off with a fistful of awards for design and content. When Bruce returned to Toronto one night to pick up the awards before all his old drinking buddies at the National Magazine Awards banquet, it was like Hannibal coming over the Alps.

Bruce's daring is matched at the other end of the country by *Alberta Report*, the only provincial weekly newsmagazine in the country. It is put out by Ted Byfield, a true believer whose editorials on Trudeau have to be typed while he's wearing asbestos gloves. So violent is he in his condemnation of Ottawa and its goofy energy policies that the pages of his magazine sometimes crinkle in the heat. Anyone in Ottawa who wants to understand Alberta's siege mentality would be wise to read it. No one in Ottawa reads it.

There is Premier John Buchanan, lighter than air, and his hairdresser. Don't leave home without one. Nova Scotia is the sump hole of Canadian tax dollars, where DREE grants speckle the hillside like sheep in Kent.

In the Just Society, Trudeau's 1968 election platform, Trudeau stated, "We must strike at the root of economic disparity, putting behind us the easy subsidized solutions of the past."

The answer was going to be the Department of Regional Economic Expansion, a munificent Santa Claus trailing goodies from Ottawa's basket. The economy would be reformed and unemployment would disappear. As with most Ottawa plans, helped by Liberal muddling, the New Jerusalem did not appear.

What happened is that last year every man, woman and child in Nova Scotia received the equivalent of $66.71 in DREE grants — easily enough to enable each citizen of the province to purchase the three volumes of *The Collected Wit of Herb Gray*. (The DREE grants per capita were $265.56 in Prince Edward Island; $8.51 for every Albertan.)

What happened is that a certain G. McClure joined DREE in 1969. He was director of operations for the East (Atlantic). During his tenure, there were three grants approved for McCain Foods Ltd., run by the millionaire McCain family of New Brunswick who have built an empire on frozen french-fried potatoes and sell McCain products all over the world. The grants totalled $7,772,221. After seventeen months, McClure left DREE to join McCain Foods in a senior capacity.

What happened is that two officers of DREE were suspended without pay in connection with a grant of $736,970 to Silver Shields Mines. The suspensions related to the officials' purchase of stock "at a moment when it was not felt to be proper."

What happened is that Jean Marchand, now Speaker of the Senate, was ultimately responsible for all DREE decisions when he was the minister in charge of the department in the early 1970s. He was also at the time the leader of the federal Liberal party in Quebec. As the 1972 election approached, Quebec's share of DREE grants moved from 36.8 percent of the Canadian total to 74.8 percent of the total.

What happened is that the grants went not only to such deserving paupers as the McCains but to other welfare cases like Michelin ($15 million for starters), Rayonnier Quebec-ITT ($14 million), Noranda Mines, Procter & Gamble, IBM and so on down the breadline.

When a Dr. Springate from the Harvard School of Business testified before the Commons committee on regional development, the government didn't like his findings. After an exhaustive investigation of a sampling of DREE grant recipients, he found that the effect of the grant program on investment decisions was small: "Movement of location of plants within Canada is minimal, and significantly, grants produce few changes in respect to project timing, project size or technology used."

His verdict: "Roughly half of the incentive grants do not influence investment in any significant manner, and can be considered to be windfall gains."

The Economic Council of Canada has been even harder on this boondoggle that Liberal ministers use, while buying votes through employment promises, to ladle out cash to the corporate welfare bums. In 1977 the council did a self-confessedly generous assessment. It found that DREE's only certain effect was to replace private investment with public money.

"Since most of the projects would have taken place somewhere in Canada if they had not been influenced to locate in particular areas by DREE," the council reported, "there appears to be a loss of real production to the economy as a whole, roughly equal to the amount of DREE money expended."

The study found that, in fact, only about *one-quarter* of DREE grants lived up to the department's mandate to encourage only investments that would otherwise not have been made.

You will be glad to know, gentle reader, that since the program began in 1969, more than $500 billion has been spent on these "incentives."

The Liberals keep pumping subsidies into obsolete steel mills and heavy water plants, and all we get back is Allan MacEachen. It doesn't seem a fair trade. Halifax is about to be accepted into the Canadian Football League. This is expected to help the cocaine dealers in town. The annual rainfall in Halifax is higher than that in Vancouver but no one mentions it — 1405.0 mm for Halifax to 1068.1 mm for Vancouver. No one, in fact, mentions Halifax. We do not plan to start.

There was that delicious moment in the autumn of 1981

when the Liberal inner cabinet travelled to Cape Breton, a junket designed to show off Allan MacEachen in his own riding. Away from the safe ghetto of Ottawa, the startled figure of External Affairs Minister Mark MacGuigan was accosted by striking coal miners, who had been out for nine weeks and demanded to know what *his* annual salary was. MacGuigan, who seems to wander through the world of diplomacy like little boy lost, is so guileless that — unlike most politicians — he sometimes blurts out the truth by accident. He confessed first of all that he didn't even know there was a strike (delicious!) and then — oh, frabjous joy! — that he couldn't remember how much he was paid. (It was $74,000 a year at the time, but now it's up to $102,100.) One wanted to be a miner at that point.

There was the helpless and bewildered look on the faces of MacEachen and Treasury Board President Don Johnston when their large car was trapped and encircled by irate miners threatening harm. Poor MacEachen, proudly hosting the think tank in his hard-times riding, was so out of touch as to be completely unprepared for the demonstrations and so led his complacent and oblivious colleagues into the ambush — and nationally televised embarrassment. Away from their warm cocoon of Ottawa, they all appear uncomfortable, as if walking on sharp stones in their bare feet.

Prince Edward Island

There is preposterous Prince Edward Island, the islet masquerading as a province. The population is 124,300, approximately the same as that of St. Catharine's, Ont. And Longueuil, Que. However, it still has four senators; British Columbia has six. This is known as co-operative federalism. P.E.I. is the home of the CBC's Mike Duffy, who is larger than three of the beaches. No one can remember the name of the premier. Millions of Canadians are born, go through life and die without ever knowing the name of the premier of Prince Edward Island. His time to speak at federal-provincial conferences is the signal for the press to go out for a beer.

Charlottetown, of course, is the home of Confederation. When this country was stillborn in 1867, foreign observers remarked on the remarkable potential ahead. Here was a land that had the fortune to be based on the solidity of the British parliamentary system, with the injection of French culture and American efficiency. It's 115 years later and what do we have? A Canada with the stability of the French political system, with American culture and British efficiency.

Charlottetown is also the place where little Jimmy Coutts, Trudeau's principal secretary, broke into tears backstage while listening to the prime minister make one of his final speeches before losing the 1979 election to Joe Clark. The tears were thought to come because Coutts had just received his private polling update from Toronto revealing that his steed was about to founder.

Coutts is from Nanton ("The finest water in Canada," proclaims a plaque on the main street), a little town just seventeen miles from Clark's High River, and went to the University of Alberta with Joe, where he was the author of the now celebrated assessment that "In this game you have to be a bit of a sonofabitch. Joe doesn't quite have it." Coutts is also widely credited in Ottawa with originating the "wimp" appellation for Clark. He denies it, but the jury is still out. (There are those who think the goal of Coutts, before tripping on his shoelaces in Toronto Spadina, was to succeed his boss Trudeau as leader, thus putting Nanton up against High River in a Huck Finn confrontation. No one, not even in P.E.I., takes Coutts' ambitions seriously.) It is not known what Clark — who, contrary to popular opinion, has a nice dry and wry wit in private — calls Mr. Coutts among intimates. Imagination, however, is rife and suggestions will be entertained for the contest.

I digress. Prince Edward Island is the second province that floats.

New Brunswick

New Brunswick is noted mainly as the refuge of two people, Richard Hatfield and Dalton Camp. Hatfield is the only bachelor among our premiers, which is unusual because they usually populate Ottawa and in fact have run this country for more than one-third of this century, of which more later. Premier Hatfield is said to be the only Canadian who receives invitations to Truman Capote's parties and can spot a good restaurant at a thousand paces. He spends so much of his time in Morocco, New York, Montreal and London that the Liberal opposition once did some research and raised the point in the legislature that the premier had spent 168 days out of the province the previous year. His friend Camp claims that Hatfield told an associate, "I was elected to run New Brunswick. No one said I had to *live* there."

Hatfield is the best leak at federal-provincial conferences. Often you will see emissaries from *As It Happens*, *Morningside*, the *Globe and Mail*, Southam News, Canadian Press, *The National* and *The Journal* lined up outside his hotel suite, being issued numbers as in a butcher shop so they can all get their own version of the truth. The other premiers tend to shun him, mainly because their wives can't figure him out and do not know how to cope with the charm and the boyish wit.

He loves parties and has a beautiful home in Fredericton filled with soft furniture. The other premiers think it is so as to accommodate his brain.

New Brunswick is also the home of Romeo LeBlanc, the Trudeaucratic minister of fisheries, a nice man who has wandered into the wrong field of work in that he is required, in return for groceries, to wobble, muddify and indulge in fuzzification — all requirements of Liberal ministers who want to earn their spurs.

Romeo used to be Trudeau's press secretary, in charge of the care and feeding of the press, and has now graduated to being the chap responsible for the slaughter of seal pups, there being a certain similarity in the two chores.

LeBlanc is a serious man, as he should be. He was formerly with the CBC in Washington, which would make a serious person out of anyone — with the possible exception of Bob Kaplan. He has the perpetual mien of a doleful spaniel on Friday the thirteenth. This may be due partially to the fact that he represents the dilemma of the country: he is Acadian, representing one-third of the province that is a perfect replica of Canada in that it also has a diminishing third of its population of French-speaking origin.

His problem is that he is trapped in an impossible dream. As a minister from the Maritimes, in charge of a traditionally Maritimes portfolio (the fishery aspect of B.C. is regarded in Ottawa as goldfish decorating hot-tubs), he must defend the indefensible: the antediluvian seal harvest.

To protect it, Romeo LeBlanc is forced into the embarrassing position of arresting Canadians — the pacifists of the Greenpeace movement — who are trying to protect Canadian seals from "harvesters" (one of the great words of our time).

The situation remains, while world opinion presses in, that for the benefit of the fashion industry the seal "harvest" is the only animal kill in the world that is conducted while the mother of the species is nursing. It will be stopped. It's simply a matter of time. Perhaps that's why Romeo looks so doleful.

This spring the New Brunswick legislature, spurred by community anger over sex acts being performed in licensed lounges by strippers and customers, assumed broad new powers to clean up the bars. At issue were lounges in two rural communities which featured strippers who mingled with the audience during their performances or performed oral sex acts.

Church groups, businessmen and women's groups in Perth-Andover and Edmundston had complained to their town councils and legislative members that the sex shows were an affront to community standards of acceptable moral behaviour.

Given royal assent, Bill 69 empowered the New Brunswick Liquor Licensing Board to suspend or revoke liquor permits if it found an establishment guilty of offering indecent, immoral or obscene entertainment.

New Brunswick also produced K. C. Irving and W. A. C. Bennett and raised Charles Lynch, though it shouldn't be held responsible for this. Most millionaires are humourless, but Irving pushes it to the breaking point. It is rumoured he last smiled in 1937. He is so silent that there is one school of thought in New Brunswick that he, like Howard Hughes, is dead but, because of his personality, they can't tell. He will never make Bartlett's.

Camp might. Any man who can tell us that when Richard Nixon proclaimed, "I am not a crook," he immediately became the "only American president in history to insist he was not a crook and tell a lie at the same time" is obviously too useful for hand-to-hand political combat.

Dalton Camp is the Typhoid Mary of Canadian politics, the smartest man in the Conservative party who is forbidden to go near it. He is, thanks to the Diefenbaker legacy, regarded as diseased, and distinguished members of the party cross the street for fear of being seen shaking his hand. Candidates for any high Tory office palpitate if it is bruited about that Camp has anything good to say about them.

Camp sits in his high wood-and-glass home in a lonely field overlooking the soft water in Queens County, thirty-six miles southeast of Fredericton, contemplating with some bemusement, mixed with amusement, the factors that have placed him here in exile, forbidden by group-think to participate in the affairs of the party he loves and despairs of. Dief, the most vindictive man in recent political time, in death has his revenge: Camp, like the Flying Dutchman, can never come home.

Camp's sin, of course, is that he forced on his party the principle of leadership review, a sacrilegious insight in 1966 but now accepted by all three parties as a natural right (and carried to such an extreme elsewhere that the newborn Social Democratic Party in Britain elected Roy Jenkins as leader by a mail vote of all card-carrying party members).

A man of no modesty but much insight, he no doubt has

contemplated one of the more amusing facets of this endlessly amusing country. The Atlantic provinces, which are the poorest of all, seldom make a noise in their indentured poverty while Western Canada, rolling in riches, screams the loudest. (Ontario merely purrs, while Quebec, knowing the real priorities, studies the Expos' box scores.)

2
Quebec
Divorce with Bed Privileges

Belgium-on-the-St. Lawrence...
the stale feud between René and Pierre...
orphans of the constitution...
Ryan won't bet on Canada's future...
slip sliding away

Being basically complacent, and a trifle tardy in tolerance, the Anglophone majority in the country makes a terrible blunder on Quebec. (The Anglo-saxophones, the ethnics, can be forgiven a bit, since they feel left out, the ignored bystanders in an old battle.) The mistake is in thinking that the leaders of the Parti Québécois, who want to take Quebec out of Canada, are narrow little men, inward-looking provincial nationalists who cannot see the vision of a larger country.

In fact, the problem is the opposite. *Our* problem, those of us who would like to see this funny collection of fiefdoms hang together, is that the Péquiste leaders are not inward-looking. They are sophisticated outward-looking politicians whose minds and philosophies have been shaped outside Canada. Their thinking was formed abroad and their political models are drawn from abroad.

All of us are products of our backgrounds, and the PQ leaders are products of their international education. They have no real experience of Canada as a country and have no interest in it. Once when I was discussing this with Claude Ryan, then still editor of *Le Devoir*, he pointed out that he had editorial writers at his paper, the most prestigious intellectual newspaper in the country, who had never been to Toronto and had no desire ever to go there. This no doubt will cause an astonishing zoom in *Le Devoir*'s circulation in Moose Jaw and Medicine Hat, but the point is useful. (Ryan, unfortunately, succumbed to the constant peril of the editorial writer — omniscience — and entered politics itself, subsequently proving, as a wise man once said, that any journalist becoming a politician is like a jockey wanting to become a horse.)

When I argue with the Parti Québécois ministers as to the inadvisability of separation, they invariably point to Sweden, with a population of 8.3 million, or Belgium with 9.9 million, or Norway with 4.1 million. Quebec, with a population of 6.4 million, has more resources, more potential, they argue. Why couldn't it survive alone? They draw their examples from the European Common Market, from international analogies.

That is where their background lies. Take a look at the international aspects of the educations of the original PQ cabinet:

Jacques-Yvan Morin: Harvard University and
      Cambridge University
Jacques Parizeau: London School of Economics
Claude Morin: Columbia University
Bernard Landry: University of Paris
Denis Lazure: University of Pennsylvania
Jacques Couture: Speaks Chinese
Louis O'Neill: Theology degree from the Vatican
Yves Berube: Massachusetts Institute of Technology

René Lévesque himself, the world's greatest advertisement for lung cancer, the tiny man in the grubby raincoat with the paster-downer hairstyle, is still underestimated by the rest of Canada. He has been around for so long, puffing into our television screens, so long thought of as an ex-journalist who hit it lucky, that his gifts are overlooked.

He is not just a hothouse nationalist, but a man with an international background equal to that of — and perhaps surpassing — *any* Canadian politician. He obviously could have been a brilliant lawyer (his father was), but he was told to leave his third-year law class at Laval and not to return

34

until he refrained from (wait for it) smoking. The law professor who issued the order was Louis-Philippe Pigeon, later a prickly justice of the Supreme Court of Canada.

Lévesque, instead, joined the U.S. Army as a war correspondent. (Those of us who delight in such things note that Lévesque, the man who wants to take Quebec out of Canada, served in the war for another country while the man who wants to keep it in, Pierre Trudeau, served not at all.)

Lévesque had a very good war. He went through the Blitz in London with Edward R. Murrow, William Shirer, Walter Cronkite and the other legendary correspondents. He crossed the Rhine with General Patton, and he saw the dead body of Benito Mussolini hanging by the heels in a Milan square. He was one of the first reporters into the Dachau death camp. He interviewed many of the top Nazi generals at the end of the war. Later, he travelled to Moscow with Lester Pearson, representing the CBC, and met Nikita Khrushchev. He was Canada's premier war correspondent in the Korean War while still in the employ of the CBC. He covered the royal tour of the Princess Elizabeth who now, as Queen of England, embodies the link that infuriates him (as it would infuriate any Anglo-Canadian if we had a French-speaking Queen living in Paris.)

On his celebrated Quebec TV show, *Point de Mire*, which thrust him into the limelight so much as to induce the vault into politics, he ranged the world and explained it for his fascinated viewers. Mistaken though his cause may be, he is the finest communicator in Canadian politics.

Pierre Trudeau ranged the world as a young man, but as a well-off gypsy, seeking esoteric revolutions and prankish escapades. There was never any danger of a cheque bouncing. Lévesque's way of seeing the world was in a rather more practical, realistic fashion. Their stars were crossed from the beginning.

There is an amusing flashback clip of Lévesque, the journalist turned politician, being interviewed on TV by a CBC team composed of Larry Zolf and one Pierre Trudeau, who said little and toyed with his notes.

Lévesque nearly slapped Trudeau in a heated argument that broke up in disorder at Jean Marchand's apartment in those heady days when a small coterie of Quebec intellectuals were anticipating the day when the witch Duplessis would be dead. There was André Laurendeau, Pelletier, Trudeau, Jean Marchand and the tentatively accepted newcomer Lévesque, who struck sparks from Trudeau from the moment they met.

The Lévesque-Trudeau relationship was formed early. When Lévesque approached the *Cité Libre* group with the idea of being a contributor, Trudeau loftily asked whether the man who had just been through a war as a U.S. war correspondent "could write."

The antagonism was natural. Lévesque, for all his world-weary appearance, is not an urban animal. He was raised closer to Halifax than Montreal, on the underbelly of the Gaspé Peninsula in the English-monikered town of New Carlisle. It was no surprise that the chain-smoking, rumpled little journalist did not hit it off with the elegant millionaire's son who had dabbled at being a professional student for so long and always wore his intellectual arrogance on a well-tailored sleeve.

We are all now captives of this stale feud. We can only wait, hoping, for one or both to leave the stage. It is rather like a visitor from Mars arriving in the United States and finding that Texas wishes to secede from the union. He then discovers, to his puzzlement, that the two major figures fighting it out are both from Texas. It just wouldn't make sense to the Martian — and it doesn't to the average Canadian.

In the Paul Sauvé Arena in east-end Montreal, six days before the 20 May 1980 separation referendum, the Pierre Elliott Trudeau who can be so good sometimes on the platform and so bad so often put on a brilliant performance. He had an overflow crowd of ten thousand federalists screaming in flag-waving passion as he replied to the Lévesque slur to foreign journalists that Trudeau wasn't really a French-Canadian because of that Elliott in his name.

He traced his Trudeau roots back to the seventeenth century, with his Elliott roots, from his mother's side, almost as long. The Elliotts, he cried, were every bit as much a part of Quebec history as the Trudeaus. He thrashed the petulant Lévesque on that point.

But Trudeau did something else in that same speech. He promised Quebec — as all the headlines recorded the next day — that the reward for a "No" vote in the referendum would be a new constitution. That is the basis for the bitterness, the sense of betrayal that rests in Quebec. When the new constitution came, Quebec was excluded — its premier undisturbed in his sleep while the middle-of-the-night deal was cooked up without him.

The original purpose of the constitution was to lay down new principles, practices and structures that would renew Canadian federalism. The principles were summarized as "pre-eminence of citizens and of their freedoms . . . full respect of native rights . . . full development of two linguistic majorities . . . enhancement of the mosaic of cultures . . . self-development of regions . . . fostering economic integration . . . promoting national solidarity . . . interdependence of two orders of government . . . strengthening of Canada as a united country to serve all Canadians."

Yet, when it was finally patched together with Scotch tape and binder twine, the native peoples opted out and today still cling to Britain as guarantor of their rights, since they have no faith in Ottawa.

The clause on women's rights was forced through only at the last moment.

Property rights were left out in deference to Prince Edward Island.

Some basic legal rights were left out.

And Quebec was left out.

From Quebec's point of view, the push toward patriation of the constitution was always based on the belief that the new constitution would grant Quebec specified powers. Daniel Johnson in 1967 spoke of the need to "establish a new sharing of powers and of resources." In the same year the constitutional committee of the Liberal party referred in its report to "the collective personality of Quebec" and put forward a long list of the powers needed to nurture that personality.

It was Expo year, the hundredth anniversary of the babe of a nation, and Lévesque, still a Liberal then, spoke in Vancouver of a Quebec stifling in "an aging and obsolete Confederation." He said it will "either become an associate state within Canada, with a special status giving it the economic, political and cultural powers required for its expansion as a nation," or else it will become independent.

Trudeau, the new prime minister in 1968, of course always opposed special status for Quebec and instead wanted to expand the constitutional rights of the French language throughout Canada.

In 1971 when Robert Bourassa scuttled the Victoria Conference, Claude Ryan as editor of *Le Devoir* wrote, "There will be no agreement forthcoming from Quebec on an amending formula or patriation without firm assurances that Quebec's key jurisdictional demands will also be included in a new constitution."

With his regained majority in 1974, Trudeau reopened his constitutional "can of worms," but by 1976 it was Bourassa who had put together a common front among premiers, opposing patriation without a substantial transfer of powers. Lévesque carried on rallying the premiers on the same issue until the 1980 forty-sixty loss on the referendum destroyed his momentum. The feds took the stance that they, not Lévesque, spoke for Quebec, an artful piece of conceit that worked until the Parti Québécois had its mandate renewed at the polls.

Such was the provincial and public distaste for the crazy Trudeau attempt to push through patriation unilaterally that Quebec was accepted as a full member of the Gang of Eight that set out to block it. The Supreme Court ruled they were correct, advising the prime minister that his initiative was legal but "unconstitutional in a conventional sense."

The eventual dog's breakfast of a Kitchen Constitution,

patched together in the early morning hours while Lévesque slept, was not liked even by the prime minister. To him, it was an "abject failure."

He should know. He brought it on himself. The man who tried an end run on the provinces and most of public opinion at the finish was on the retreat, the premiers having cornered him through patience (with a little help from Bora and the Supremes).

The whole noble act of creation of a nation's constitution got down to 3:30 AM haggling in a hotel bedroom. All it needed was a private eye on a ladder outside the window of the Château Laurier and the farce would have been complete. A constitution born of adultery.

Pierre Trudeau's concept of nation-building is a peculiar one. The man who came to Ottawa in the first place to keep Quebec within Confederation and to preserve a country decided to cap his career by going to war with the provinces and alienating most of the premiers with whom he had to work. Because the patriation of the constitution (from its silly resting spot across an ocean in the hands of a foreign nation) was the ultimate target of his whole political career, he decided to achieve it by insulting the heads of the provinces, belittling them and calling them mere horse traders.

The result of all this? On that final panic-stricken night in Ottawa, with politicians ricocheting from suite to suite like confused swains in a French comedy, the high-minded feds ended up wheeling and dealing with those despised premiers in a scene that resembled the Casablanca carpet-dealers' convention. Swap this. Swap that. Override this. Override that. This is the way a country is born. Not in full view of the public, as the proud (and more democratic) Americans would have demanded in similar circumstances, but at 3:30 AM in Allan Blakeney's bedroom.

Pierre Trudeau's stubborn vow that he would go to Westminster alone was never going to work. His insistence on deadlines (to fit in with his own personal plans for retirement) was never going to work. His claim that he was justified in acting unilaterally because patriation had been stalled for fifty-four years was nonsense. The usual intellectual flim-flam. The voters had become interested in the issue only in the previous three years, and public opinion had slowly coalesced (to be ignored after midnight in hotel rooms).

We were getting there, in our own fuddling and delaying Canadian way. What the public did not count on was a clutch of conspirators tossing out human rights in all-night sessions like spare cabbages too heavy for the shopping basket.

How is a country built? After the miles of constitutional lawyers have unravelled their tongues? The present unsatisfactory solution comes, partially from a chance meeting between the Saskatchewan and Ontario premiers and their aides in an Ottawa Italian restaurant. A Magna Carta on a checkered tablecloth. Watch the tomato sauce. Wouldn't want it to drip on women's rights.

How is a country built? The Kitchen Constitution that formed the basis for the patchwork compromise that formed the deal that drove Quebec closer to separation that put the sieve in the house that Sir John A. built? Scribbled on bits of paper in a spare pantry, Casablanca rug merchants dealing trades with those who can stay the course.

How is a country built? In that late night in November 1980, proudly announced to the populace on the telly the next morning. Manitoba's Sterling Lyon was no longer there, gone home to put the finishing touches on losing an election. B.C.'s Bill Bennett, a nonlawyer, exhausted at the legal bafflegab, had gone to his pillow, leaving aides to "bargain." P.E.I.'s Angus MacLean, retiring in a few days, wasn't a factor. The fixers from Ontario, Alberta, Saskatchewan and Newfoundland didn't even bother waking René Lévesque, their companion in the long struggle of the Gang of Eight, to inform him that they were settling the flea market. That's the way a country is built, a Rube Goldberg bleary-eyed creation that came apart almost immediately.

The prime minister, in his contempt for the premiers, always maintained their concept of the constitution didn't extend beyond swapping "fish" for "oil." In the end, he did something worse. He swapped human rights like rugs.

40

The fifty percent of the population that is female? Out the window — forced back in only because of the outcry. Native rights? Out. The Château Laurier was turned into Casablanca because of — as the Supreme Court hinted — Pierre Trudeau's basic lack of understanding of what democracy is all about.

On 16 April 1982, the day before Queen Elizabeth (whose coronation René Lévesque had covered as an employee of a crown corporation) proclaimed on Parliament Hill the constitution that left out one-quarter of Canada, the premier of Quebec said, "We must refuse clearly to be more and more of a minority, more and more dependent, less and less significant. We must decide for ourselves soon — before it is too late — to affirm at least the majority that we are here in Quebec, to decide that Quebec must belong to us . . . as a country, a real country where we can be truly at home."

The Trudeau gamble in becoming the father of a constitution that leaves out his own province is that the Parti Québécois is a mere passing aberration that will fade away so that he or his heirs will then be able to negotiate with a more amenable Quebec government.

It's a great theory. But what if he is wrong?

Separatism wasn't "dead" as he predicted, and the PQ wasn't dead after losing the referendum. After fourteen years, Trudeau has no monopoly on wisdom pertaining to the province that raised him.

Even his fellow Liberal, Claude Ryan, thinks the surprisingly complacent way that Trudeau gave in on the constitution, after his long autocratic stance, makes the breakup of Confederation more likely.

Writing in the summer issue of *Policy Options*, a political science journal, the disillusioned and beleaguered Quebec Liberal leader — before he resigned — concluded, "Mr. Trudeau wanted to reinforce Canadian federalism. On the contrary, what he has done threatens to weaken it where it most urgently needs reinforcement — in Quebec."

Ryan gloomily predicted that the constitutional events of 1982 had given Lévesque's party's argument for independence "the new inspiration it sorely needed. The Parti Québécois predicted things would get worse (in the event of a referendum defeat), and now it can point out that things are getting worse and it's happening in front of our eyes."

By getting the provinces to go along with his idea of Canada, Trudeau had asked Quebec to accept the English-Canadian national image of an independent country "developing in the shadow of the British monarchy."

That does nothing to convince nationalist Quebecers that Canada is their country and "If the prospects of Canada rest on such an artificial foundation, I wouldn't bet much on its future."

Pierre Trudeau previously humiliated an earlier Quebec Liberal premier, Robert Bourassa, by calling him a "hotdog" publicly. Now he is alienated completely from the intellectual Ryan. He seems not able to get along either with adversaries or allies, hotdog or egghead. He seems a strange man to bind a country together. His regard for himself gets in the way.

With Lévesque inching his province toward some sort of sovereignty-association ("Divorce with bed privileges," as Bill Bennett calls it), even the base of the Liberal party is in peril. If Quebec, in some form, goes, there go the Grits as a national party. If the PQ, as threatened, runs candidates in the next federal election, it is likely they could win the dozen or so of Quebec's seventy-five seats that would destroy any Liberal chance of forming a government in Ottawa. The strange thing is that Pierre Trudeau, who went to Ottawa in the first place so as to keep Quebec within Confederation, may both lose Quebec and destroy the Liberal party. The man who called the Liberals gutless when Lester Pearson approved nuclear weapons on Canadian soil may leave it skeleton-less.

3
First Stopover
The Sidewalks of Montreal

The essence of the city is female . . .
a display case for personality . . .
the legend of Nick Auf der Maur . . .
Mordecai Richler on a tear . . .
Drapeau's edifice complex . . . 4 A.M. traffic jams . . .
even the scandals have a flair

The most civilized of all Canadian cities is also the one where the licence plates make a political statement. Other provinces use their licence plates to boast about their tasty gooseberries or to vilify litterbugs (Can there be a more inane statement anywhere than "Keep Ontario Beautiful"?). Quebec cars, instead, are adorned with "Je Me Souviens" — I Remember. It's a serious business in a city that takes seriously the art of living well.

The essence of Montreal as a city is *female*. Toronto is male. (Vancouver is androgynous and Ottawa is indexed.) Montreal is proud, a show-off, extravagant, vainglorious, impractical and elegant. There is a sense, on the streets, that one is on stage, auditioning for the eyes of all others. Pedestrians do not strut so much as parade. A stroll along Sherbrooke Street is still the finest visual feast in the country, the best-dressed women (Toronto's Bloor Street-Hazelton Lanes enclave is too self-consciously stylish), the most calmly confident men. There is on Montreal streets a bit of the Roman's gift for using the sidewalks as a display case for personality. Other Canadian cities use sidewalks as a thoroughfare for foot traffic; Montreal uses them for entertainment.

It is a city that has been ruled in secrecy for a quarter century by a man who even gets ill in secrecy. Mayor Jean

Drapeau, probably the most skilled politician in Canada, has run the city imperiously, with one short interruption, for twenty-five years. When he entered hospital this summer, it was four days before the public was informed he had had a stroke.

He does not give press conferences. He does not speak to reporters, only to his biographers. His stay in hospital was his first "holiday" in twenty-five years. Late at night he likes to drive about the city at great speed by himself, classical music blasting from his stereo. He has emerged unscathed from the greatest public scandal of our time: the disgrace and corruption in the building of the Olympic Stadium. (Vancouver in 1983 will open Canada's first domed stadium; the total cost of $125 million will be less than what it will take to finish the Olympic Stadium roof, with no one yet certain whether it will work.)

(Why is the federal Liberal party like the Big Owe? Because it has a deficit, a large hole in the middle of it and an uncertain future. I digress.)

There is the institution of the Ritz-Carlton, reigning over Sherbrooke Street, home of the Bar Mitzvahs and the five o'clock assignations in the bar, where the nuts are irresistible. Sunday brunch in the Ritz garden, with the *New York Times*, the white ducks paddling in the pond, is one of the more civilized activities in a world filled with plane hijackers, punk rock and the Canadian postal service. (At the end of the summer, the hotel kills the ducks and serves them up.) There is a sedate ritual in the Ritz bar in late afternoon, when preserved-in-aspic matrons from the Westmount ghetto come down the Mount Royal slope and sit quietly over a drink, contemplating past glories. There is in the scene a cameo out of another institution, the Meikles Hotel in Salisbury, now Harare, in Rhodesia, now Zimbabwe, where the patrons seem to be part of the furniture and looking backward over time.

The Ritz is handy. Mordecai Richler's apartment is right across the street. So is Brian Mulroney's office. The Maritime Bar downstairs, once the most comfortable lunch spot in town, hasn't the appeal since it has been redecorated. Some museums need to be preserved.

What sets Montreal apart is the slight air of late-1920s New York to it. There are still *boulevardiers* in Montreal, bon vivants who squeeze every last bit out of the night. One of them is Nick Auf der Maur, a near-legend in his own time, a journalist and politician and provocateur. Living well, as the countess said, is the best revenge, and Auf der Maur follows the principle, sometimes too well. He charts the changing drinking patterns of the Crescent Street regulars in his Montreal Gazette column as assiduously as a chess master, and bistros fall and prosper on his scouting reports.

He was one of the hordes arrested in the War Measures swoop, an event that has enhanced his career, like someone who has had a good war. As an opposition member of the city council that Drapeau ignores, he wrote a fabulously detailed book on all the Olympic corruption that later formal inquiries confirmed. The Los Angeles 1984 Olympic Games organizers have flown him in to hear his warnings on overspending. He calls himself "the Red Adair of the Olympics movement."

He has a fine mind topped with a manic wit, separated only by a healthy thirst. He is a Montreal original and could not be transplanted anywhere else. His flower would wither and die.

Richler, especially while on a tear, is a *boulevardier* of another stance, a gifted writer who has made a career of mocking his upbringing in the Jewish ambience of St. Urbain street across town. He no longer speaks with his mother and enjoys life in his own bittersweet way. He grows out of the Montreal pavement and he, too, could never be dug up and grafted elsewhere. Montreal has this peculiar early-New-York sense, of producing characters who could not possibly *fit* anywhere else. Only Vancouver is similar in this way, in creating some people who would expire from culture shock if shifted to a foreign (i.e., across the mountains) ambience.

Montreal is the only Canadian city with 4 AM traffic jams. The 4 AM traffic jams are filled with Mercedes-Benz taxi cabs. The centre of street life has shifted recently from the boutique-and-bistro glitter of Crescent Street one block west to Bishop, where the midnight air is filled with BMWs, silk and young men with expense account hair.

After the Parti Québécois came to power, the emboldened separatist youth decided to reclaim their own city and established a rival café society on St. Denis, which is the demarcation line to the east end of city where Drapeau's voters live and love his grandiose edifice complex. On St. Jean Baptiste night, two cultures now compete in street theatre, the true party-goers drifting from rival camp to rival camp. The gonzo successor to St. Urbain's Horseman will be written by someone who can translate that rivalry into an explanation of the new Montreal, financially wounded by the Anglo Boat People taking the 401 escape to Toronto, but being reborn in a more self-controlled way.

Montreal, the home of Pierre Trudeau, has traffic signs that now — unlike Paris — do not say: Arrêt/Stop. It is only Arrêt, thanks to the language police of Bill 101, the tongue-troopers. As Lévesque himself says, he was "humiliated" at having to bring in such a bill, but he had to save Montreal, the second-largest French-speaking city in the world, from becoming an English-speaking city. If Montreal fell, there would be no hope for the rest of the province.

There has never been a situation where a minority acting as if it were a majority did not invite revenge. The Westmount Rhodesians did exploit their comfortable position in Quebec society, and now the revenge-mongers, led by the Grim Reaper Dr. Camille Laurin, are having their innings. Logic will prevail, in the end, but for the moment we must endure the vengeance. Generations have long memories.

The most telling example of how deep runs the bitterness against the slights of the Westmount Rhodesians was the farce of Claude Charron, Lévesque's mercurial House leader, stealing a $130 tweed jacket from Eaton's in downtown Montreal. The department store, no doubt realizing the political implications in the light of the flight of Anglophones from the city, pondered long and hard and went through all the precautionary formalities before filing shoplifting charges.

48

Immediately — helped along by Lévesque's rather dishonest hints — there was the Francophone outcry of persecution ordered by the "bosses" in Toronto. (The decision to proceed on the charges was made by Francophone executives of Eaton's in Montreal.) While the threats and the hot-lines hummed, it turned out that this was no mere absentminded shoplifter but a cabinet minister who, when questioned at the door, fled for blocks, leaping traffic barricades and risking death by dodging speeding cars before being wrestled to earth by a security guard.

The accusations of Anglo "persecution" of a pure and simple thief were finally silenced by a telling little letter to a Montreal paper by a French-Canadian boy who said that what he apparently was being advised was that it was wrong to steal from French stores but it was okay to steal from English stores. The silence was deafening. And a little child may lead them. . . .

Speaking of that, the single most important player in the Canadian Football League in 1982 is Luc Tousignant, the Trois-Rivières native who was given a chance to quarterback the born-again Montreal Concorde. He is the first chance for the Québécois to shape their own hero and save a franchise in the biggest stadium in Canada (after the club was pillaged and near-ruined by the offhand management of Vancouver buccaneer Nelson Skalbania). Cool Hand Luc was the key to attendance figures — and keeping Montreal in the CFL instead of defecting to Drapeau's dream, a National Football League franchise.

Drapeau dreams Montreal's dreams. He knows his flock well. He has conditioned them to world standards: Expo '67, the Olympic Games, a showcase subway system, a pioneering subterranean shopping and pedestrian maze. He likes the flamboyant and so does Montreal. Even the scandals have a flair: Lévesque runs over a drunk, Charron steals a sports jacket, Olympic Stadium gravel truck operators drive in one gate and out another, collecting their fee without ever dumping their load and drive around again. *Insouciance* counts in Montreal. Actor Donald Sutherland, the Number One Expos baseball freak, was in Paris during a crucial July series with league-leading St. Louis. He phoned a friend and listened, across the Atlantic, to the games.

Montreal doesn't abide losers (Toronto shrugs and goes back to the money) which is why the Montreal Canadien players dread a summer on the golf course when they don't win the Stanley Cup, having to explain *why* day after endless day on the green. Which is why the city, currently shifting its cultural base from being tenant to being owner, will be a winner again. Trust me.

4
First Digression

Trudeau's Cabinet
or
Journey to the Land of Nod

Pierre Elliott Reincarnation
and his feckless disciples . . .
Chrétien confides in Fodderingham . . .
an agriculture minister with
foot in mouth disease . . . Senator Phogbound

Pierre Trudeau, despite the famed reputation for steely discipline and iron command, is, in fact, a lousy leader. In his airy hubris he has driven/scared/sluffed off all the strong Anglos who once populated his ministry. He is the neutron bomb of Liberal politics, destroying all the personalities within while leaving the institution standing (barely).

Paul Hellyer, as a stiff-principled housing minister after forcing all the Canadian armed forces to look like Coca-Cola deliverymen, marched into Mr. Trudeau's office threatening to resign and had the offer ripped out of his hand so fast his church-choir baritone is still squeaky. John Turner went into Mr. Trudeau's office to discuss a promised relief from the dead-end finance portfolio and — after being insulted by being offered the Senate or a spot on the bench — emerged with tears in his eyes, having resigned.

The gutsy Eric Kierans left after determining that his trademark — economic honesty and bluntness — was not appreciated or wanted.

The disputatious Bryce Mackasey, who is nothing if not passionate, resigned one morning in a temper, was persuaded by advisors to recant but, unwisely, had lunch first and grew so agitated during his afternoon repentance session with the

PM that he resigned again, which is thought to be a *Guinness Book of World Records* mark for most resignations in one day. His tempestuous career, in and out of the cabinet, then a term in the Quebec legislature, an abortive try at an Ottawa seat and eventually a resting spot in the Ontario federal riding of Lincoln, on the excuse that was where his mother lived, inevitably brought forward the Press Gallery question: "Why is an Edsel running in Lincoln?"

The right-leaning Bob Andras, who wanted to be finance minister, left when he saw that the Ping-Pong Trudeau mind was about to flip into one of its nationalist left-leaning modes. He departed for corporate stamp-collecting in Vancouver.

Ron Basford, an honest toiler, left after four cabinet posts — and no one in authority wrote him a letter, thanked him or said, "In your hat."

Mr. Trudeau never dissuades anyone who offers to leave, nor does he think it his responsibility to recruit talented newcomers. Each individual is expected to survive in the vacuum in which Trudeau grooms his own intellect. He doesn't like people, but he does like money and his cheapness, as Margaret's memoirs testify, extends to worn towels and thin linen.

It is amusing that his inherited fortune began as a chain of Montreal Island gas stations which his father sold to Imperial Oil (a.k.a. Esso, a.k.a. Exxon), which ultimately became one of the multinational targets of the disastrous National Energy Policy — the latter-day Trudeau nationalist conversion that turned foreign investors against Canada and destroyed the dollar, the economy and Trudeau's place in history as a triumphant leader. The man dallied over the constitution while the buck burned.

The prime requisite of any leader — in business, politics, academe, publishing or elsewhere — is to assure that there is an acceptable and competent successor in place so as to guarantee continuity. By this criterion, Mr. Trudeau again qualifies as a lousy leader. Proof of this is that in the present Liberal frontbench, where seat assignment is designated by seniority, the man now sitting three chairs away from the prime minister of Canada is Agriculture Minister Eugene Whelan, who only takes his foot out of his mouth to change feet.

The old Ottawa line on Whelan is that he had a bad fire at his house, destroying his entire library. It burned both books and one of them he hadn't finished colouring yet. That is a canard, of course, because we have it on authority that he reads in bed every night until his lips get tired.

Such jollities, prime fodder at press gatherings, are in the same vein as the Liberal minister, well-washed in the brandy one evening, who was asked to fess up as to who the cabinet would nominate as leader "if the PM were run over by a bus tomorrow."

"Easy," was the reply. "The bus driver."

The serious part is that Pierre Trudeau, the man who won't recruit and can't retain, has basically destroyed the Liberal party as a national force. It is a regional government attempting to govern nationally. Fifty percent of the Liberal caucus in Parliament is from Quebec. If you take the Quebec factor out of Gallup Poll soundings, the Liberals are running third, behind even the NDP, in the rest of the country.

When Pierre Elliott Reincarnation came to power in 1968, Lester Pearson left him with almost half of Canada — four provinces — under Liberal rule at the provincial level. A fifth and sixth province came later. Today, of course, there is not a single province with a Liberal government.

The combination of Trudeau truculence and indifference has killed the party at the provincial level in Western Canada. In Alberta, it is as dead as the dinosaurs; it is in the grave in Saskatchewan; it is dying in Manitoba and in B.C., to paraphrase John Diefenbaker, it is protected only by the game laws. There isn't a single Liberal left in any of the four Western legislatures, and the only two Western MPs, Lloyd Axworthy and Bob Bockstael, stand almost no chance of re-election.

A further example of Mr. Trudeau's Frisbee-playing with portfolios is the solicitor-general post, thought to be a fairly important position considering its role in the criminal justice system of the country.

When Trudeau became leader in 1968, he shuffled off

George McIlraith, one of the Pearson government veterans, into the ministry. By 1970 the unforgettable Jean-Pierre Goyer — incredibly bright and incredibly accident-prone — was given the job. He lasted not two years before Trudeau, shuffling again (not cleaning house, but shuffling) put in the job the sincere and hard-working Warren Allmand.

Allmand set a record under Trudeau (perhaps why he was later bounced from the cabinet): he lasted almost four years in the portfolio.

There next came calligraphy expert Francis Fox, continuing the Trudeau practice of using this potentially dangerous legal role as a sort of training bra post for untried juniors. When Fox had to resign because of his forgetfulness in not telling his boss about personal problems, the ever-smiling Jean-Jacques Blais took over this particular deck chair on the Titanic.

Blais lasted the bare minimum of two years, ducking flak and grenades in the Commons almost every week, a pratfall looking for a place to happen, before being recycled. Bob Kaplan, who had been lusting to get into the cabinet since first being elected in the Trudeaumania sweep of 1968, finally got his reward: the ejector seat also known as solicitor-general.

This bumbling record demonstrates the anomaly in the rigid brain of Pierre Elliott Trudeau. He is famously tough on philosophy, on principles, on issues. But when it comes to changing the men who must apply those principles, he is as dishwater.

He abides to an amazing degree (some shrinks might give you another opinion) helpless victims, men who can't cross the rug without walking on their tongues. A retrospective look at Trudeau's fourteen years with such as André Ouellet and John Munro would make you weep.

Heavy-handed fumblers walking about looking for an open manhole, they foul up, resign and are accepted back into the fold in time by a master who seems, in all honesty, to be so beset by lassitude as not to have the energy to examine the rest of his flock for talent. In truth, it is easier to keep a Munro or an Ouellet around than a Turner or a Kierans. Trudeau takes the easy way out.

Yet there is an air of genial arrogance to the Liberal frontbench, the Natural Governing Party being in such general contempt of both Joe Clark's abilities and the lust of the Tory party to destroy itself that it cruises along, awash in superiority, rather like a Chrysler Air-Flow in overdrive.

Jean Chrétien, puppy-dog frisky, is the most appealing of this bunch but even he has looked somewhat tarnished in his messenger-boy role on the constitution, eager not to irritate his boss since he is attempting the audacious task of succeeding him.

Chrétien's chances of doing so, strangely enough, are being wrecked by what one would think would be his strength: the Quebec caucus. The realization has sunk in among Quebec MPs that if they put their concerted support behind Chrétien — and were successful — it would naturally shatter the unwritten Grit law that has been a key to the party's success: the switching of the leadership between Anglo and Francophone leaders. It has sunk in that if the Quebec wing of the party allows a Francophone to succeed a Francophone, it could lead to a future scenario of a Turner followed by a Macdonald followed by a Fotheringay — and how could Quebec then object?

I once put this notion to Chrétien over dinner and, in his usual irrepressible manner, he said, "Well, Fodderingham, I'll tell you a story."

The story was that Chrétien and Clark always got along well on a personal basis, perhaps because of both being barefoot kids from rather modest backgrounds. In 1975 when Clark was trying to decide if he would assay his rather audacious run at the Tory leadership, he encountered Chrétien at a urinal in the parliamentary washroom. He asked Chrétien's advice as to whether he should try it.

"Joe, I'll guarantee you only one thing," replied Chrétien. "If you don't run, you won't win."

Chrétien turned to me. "Well, Fodderingham, you may be right but I tell you, if I don't run, I won't win."

Chrétien is impossible to dislike, always looking, as Dalton Camp put it, like "the driver of the getaway car." (Cartoonists would be kinder to him if they knew that the

57

famous gangster-out-of-the-corner-of-the-mouth speaking style is because of deafness in one ear.) He is the second youngest of nineteen children, only nine of whom survived. When you come out of Shawinigan, you learn to be a street-fighter.

He is the most solidly married man in Canada. Sequestered as a teen-ager in a church school where girls were not allowed even to visit, he would spend Sunday afternoons walking, trailing fingers, with his sixteen-year-old love, she on the outside of the school fence, he inside. Chrétien arrived in Ottawa in 1963 not speaking a word of English. Adopted as a protégé by Finance Minister Mitchell Sharp, Chrétien was warned by a Quebec colleague after a meeting with high mandarins that the conversations must be regarded as confidential. "You don't have to worry," said Chrétien. "I didn't understand a goddam word."

Alone of the Quebec ministers, he has been a great hit in Western Canada (though is in danger of overdoing it) with his Johnny Baptiste act, telling delighted audiences that he is just a little "pea-souper" who puts "the em-*phas*-is on the wrong sy-*lla*-ble." In fact, he has surprising Western connections. His grandfather, fed up with something, emigrated to Alberta and corresponded with the family constantly on his Prairie experiences. There are some forty-plus Chrétien relatives sprinkled throughout Alberta, ready for the leadership battle.

The street-fighter, naturally, has always been in awe of the elegantly dressed and elegantly egoed leader from Montreal's best salons. Early in his cabinet term, Chrétien found himself in a government plane beside Trudeau on the way to a Liberal event. Struggling for conversation, Chrétien grasped upon the fact that rain had begun to sprinkle his window. "It's raining outside," he ventured helpfully.

"When it's raining, it's always outside," was the bored rejoinder from the prime minister of all Canada. The journey continued in silence.

Allan MacEachen is an explorer, a prober, a Dr. Livingstone of the oratorical art. He is a cartographer of language, someone who finds gullies, crevices, arroyos, dips and undulations on the way to the end of a sentence. He approaches a question period query as he would a bramblebush, carefully meandering his way around it, probing, poking, his fuzzy syntax taking on the qualities of a porcupine, impenetrable, unfathomable, a possible conclusion hidden in a thicket of circumlocutions.

Robert Fulford once wrote that when he listened to a Paul Martin speech he had the feeling his head was being slowly filled with glue. Listening to MacEachen masticating an answer in the House of Commons, ruminating on his choice of prevarications rather like a cow chewing on its cud before depositing it in one of the bifurcations of the stomach, is to witness a master obfuscator, one who uses the language of Shakespeare to conceal rather than to reveal. He is an ecdysiast of the encyclopedia, the Gypsy Rose Lee of the dictionary, a man so used to having his mouth filled with mush that he wouldn't recognize English if he swallowed it.

The first time I met MacEachen was 1968, in his corner station in the Ottawa ice rink, just before the opening ballot in the Liberal leadership race that went to four ballots and featured eight well-qualified candidates, plus the Rev. Lloyd Henderson. (The Rev. Lloyd, mayor of Portage La Prairie, Man., had also run for the leadership in the 1958 convention that chose Lester Pearson. He received one vote and the magnificent Norman Depoe, on national television, consoled him by saying that he at least had the satisfaction of voting for himself. "Oh, I wasn't a voting delegate," confessed Rev. Lloyd. "But my wife and mother-in-law were.")

But I digress. I was introduced to MacEachen by an old friend, Richard Vogel, who went to law school in the Maritimes. Always the diligent reporter, I immediately asked MacEachen where he was going to throw his votes when he was bounced early (as I assumed he knew he would be). Vogel, a consummate gentleman and now B.C.'s deputy attorney-general, rolled his eyes to the roof and looked away in agony, mortified at what he had anticipated would be a genial how-do-you-do introduction. MacEachen blanched and looked stricken, as if someone had told him his fly was open.

He died, of course, on the first ballot, getting only 165

votes. He was so stunned and confused that he didn't get his withdrawal to the convention chairman in time to get his name off the second ballot — which delivered him eleven votes.

It was a defeat so predictable to your scribe and so surprising to MacEachen that it later made more understandable his total misreading of his celebrated budget botch-up that ultimately ruined his career. As a result of my famed diplomacy, we did not speak again for thirteen years, until we were seated opposite one another at the 1981 Parliamentary Press Gallery banquet and could hardly avoid the niceties.

Eugene Whelan sits in the frontbench, seemingly forlorn without the green felt cowboy hat he wears whenever outdoors, and perhaps to bed. He is a large bloodhound, morose, his mangled features never changing, continuing reading his documents when even his less-enthusiastic seatmates are up on their hindlegs pounding their mitts together on some stale excuse for partisan thumping, like fraternity boys in a cafeteria, applauding something of which they know naught, but expressing the bonding of the troupe. Snuffling at the same waterhole.

Whelan keeps to himself, a warthog among dandies and triflers, tolerated by Trudeau only because, with no Western bodies available, Trudeau must appoint an Ontario agriculture minister to shepherd a portfolio that largely concerns Westerners. Meanwhile Whelan has been steadily courting farm support for his long-planned leadership bid that seems loony, but as he looks about him at some of the other pretenders, he merely shrugs, puts on his hat and goes to bed.

Jean-Luc Pépin, always looking like the comedian in a French bedroom farce, is an unhappy man, a tender poet put among dray horses. He sulks like a cocker spaniel at slights and has been subdued since Trudeau insulted him by shoving him into the meat-and-potatoes transport slot, where his professor's gifts are not exactly suited for boxcars and coal ports. Trudeau does not like him, since Pépin had constitutional ideas of his own and the PM usually does not like anyone who disagrees with him.

The Robarts-Pépin task force on the constitution (Monty

Pépin's Flying Circus), a $4,323,736 million test of the elasticity of the taxpayer's wallet, was sunk in the Rideau Canal and hasn't been seen since. Peter Lougheed, by the way, thinks Pépin is a fair person. He sits two seats to the right of Trudeau in the frontbench and they seldom speak.

Marc Lalonde, as David Crombie puts it, would pick a fight on the way to church. The most genial of companions in private, with a grin that stretches from Rimouski to Regina, in public he is the stiff-necked hit man of the Trudeau cabinet. If Chrétien looks like the driver of the getaway car, Lalonde is the guy carrying the violin case.

He shares an affliction, in a strange way, with Robert Stanfield and Joe Clark (both Clark and Lalonde started their political careers devoted to the brilliance of the tragic Davie Fulton, destroyed by Dief's vindictiveness and bounced from the B.C. bench for drunken driving). Stanfield, Clark and Lalonde are comfortable, witty companions in private, in small groups, but once some magic figure is reached — when stepping before, say, thirty people — they are transformed. The former two freeze and perform like marionettes, the latter drops his grin, shifts into his machine-gun mind and lets fire, safety catch forgotten. The first two are intimidated by crowds, the last one attempts to intimidate the world, which is usually mistaken for Alberta.

(Mr. Trudeau has the opposite problem: so engaging when he wants to be in his kiss-trampoline public persona, he is a chilly, encased intellect in private — but that's another book, that has been written thrice.)

Lalonde's lordly manner toward the unwashed comes honestly: he is a solid man whose family has farmed the same land on an island in the St. Lawrence for eight generations. Like Trudeau, he was a civil servant before being persuaded to offer his name on a ballot and so, like his master, brings a father-knows-best attitude to politics, an attitude that accounts for so much of the Liberal party's charm, panache and winsomeness.

Early in his career, Marc Lalonde vowed to rearrange a Canada where insults to French-Canadians were no longer possible. He helped Trudeau achieve that necessary goal, but his hardness, his lack of charity in public comments, has helped to divide the country on an east-west axis.

The failure of the Trudeau era is that the man went to Ottawa for the most noble of purposes, to convince Quebec that it had a place in the capital of Canada. But because of his autocratic manner, he has driven out so many men of talent from the Anglophone end of the world that he has had to appoint Lalonde to the essentially Western portfolio of energy and Pépin to the indubitably Western portfolio of transport — knowing that his only possible alternative — Lloyd Axworthy — was too callow for the task. The fault was not Axworthy's, but Trudeau's. The man who thinks recruiting is beneath him reaps the whirlwind.

He is concerned for his country but burnishing his own ego has proven, in the end, more important than his party.

His persona has come before his party. It will be up to history to judge but, one suspects, the process might have been served better if the order of precedence had been readjusted.

I digress, slightly. One of the few interesting faces in the Trudeau crew is Don Johnston, the treasury board president who was Trudeau's personal lawyer in Montreal. He retains his sanity by having a piano in his East Block office and pounds away when the political inanities get to him. The last keeper of the black and white keys in cabinet was Mitchell Sharp, who played sedately as if to fit his parliamentary style. Johnston, playing ragtime in his blue corduroy suit, resembles an antic Yukon piano player in a house of ill repute. (In fact, it's across the way, in the Centre Block.) He is gangly and looks as if he might have trouble in a crosswalk but, surprisingly is a terrific tennis player and was on the McGill team. His arms and legs go off in all directions, like Stephen Leacock's horseman, but in truth he's an athletic Joe Clark.

Mines Minister Judy Erola stands out like burnished steel, a widow with a spring in her step, who enters the House each day looking as if just scrubbed from the bath. A tough lady, she would seem to have unlimited potential if Iona Campagnolo (one of The Pretenders) were not lurking in the weeds, waiting for the call.

John Roberts, the Minister in Charge of Acid Rain, a portfolio unfitting to his drawing room gifts, no longer takes himself seriously as a leadership candidate. This is fortunate because his assessment is now attuned to the thoughts of others. What he really needs is a pair of designer gumboots.

Then there's the already mentioned "Hungry Bob" Kaplan. He has been so referred to around Ottawa after encountering, on a parliamentary elevator, Pat Carney, the vigorous Conservative MP for Vancouver Centre, which has the worst child prostitution and street sex problem in Canada. She had demanded in the Commons that the government do something about the disgrace.

On the elevator, the feckless Kaplan, solicitor-general of Canada, tells her that he can't understand her concern, since it must be good for the fast food business in the riding: "Everyone knows that when you get laid, you get hungry."

Hungry Bob, out of elevators, is painfully earnest (he is coauthor with his wife of a tome called *Bicycling in Toronto*) and walks about with an air of innocent puzzlement as to why the world is picking on him.

He defends, then doesn't defend, the RCMP opening our mail. He defends — then reveals he didn't know about — his agents paying $100,000 to a mass-murderer for telling where his corpses were buried. He is terminally stumble-tongued. Ontario County Court Judge Barry Shapiro refused to allow one of Kaplan's helpful letters — a signed character reference for an accused, one of Kaplan's constituents — to be read in court because it was in "poor taste." The judge, rightly, could see it. Kaplan couldn't.

Poor taste is not the word for our prime minister. Poor judgment in men is the proper phrase.

There are others, never-weres and never-will-be's, testaments to the curious Trudeau belief that he is neither responsible for recruiting nor retaining. He almost never sacks anyone; for a man supposedly so strong on principles, on policies, he is strangely reluctant to follow through on his logic to replace those who foul up on his assigned plan.

Those who disgrace themselves (Francis Fox, who couldn't remember his right name; André Ouellet, guilty of contempt of court; John Munro, who phoned a judge) are merely sent into the anteroom to be laundered, then resurface in the cabinet completely cleansed of the lack of judgment they were born with. Lord Carrington, the most respected member of Margaret Thatcher's cabinet, resigned over the Falklands farce as a matter of principle, because he accepted responsibility. Ministers who couldn't carry his spats lounge in Trudeau's cabinet for years and are shuffled about as in checkers. Not chess, checkers.

The unhappy Munro — perspiring, either chain-smoking or endlessly trying to quit — is the only man who has managed to make the bathtub into an offensive weapon. Fox's main accomplishment in Ottawa is still his permanent. It is hard to believe that magazine profiles once pictured the chippy and surly Ouellet as a possible French-Canadian prime minister. His famous complaint, following a disastrous post office strike, that any small businessmen who really relied on the post office for their livelihood had perhaps better find other work is already enshrined in the pantheon of Grit thought, somewhere near the level of the famous pronouncement of the beloved post office union leader Joe Davidson that "the public can go to hell." The sentiments — one from an embittered leader of post office workers, the other from the minister in charge — both came under the aegis of Liberal rule. They have set the tone. Two moronic statements fit and match.

Paul Cosgrove's political career was finished one autumn day in 1981. Angry and worried mortgage-holders, hit with the threat of foreclosures due to zooming interest rates, took a six-hour bus ride from Toronto to protest on Parliament Hill. Cosgrove, a seemingly competent municipal politician from Toronto, was taken into the cabinet as housing minister, what would seem a modest role for a newcomer to the House of Commons.

When the seven hundred middle-class demonstrators arrived on the parliamentary lawn for their orderly protest, not a single Liberal minister, let alone Housing Minister Cosgrove, had the courage or courtesy to come out and address them or accept their petitions. Further, some insensitive twit within the system ordered Mounties equipped with helmets, clubs and the usual riot gear to guard Parliament from the people who own it. A government that sends armed police against people who are merely frightened of losing their homes is not a government that deserves support.

There are such as Ed Lumley, the poor man's John Turner, and Jim Fleming who sounds like he is delivering a radio commercial (his old trade) every time he tries to issue what is meant to be an important pronouncement.

There is Herb Gray (known in the Press Club as gray Herb), as earnest as his press releases are unreadable. He is the Number One nationalist in cabinet, continually buffeted from success to defeat by Trudeau's detours of philosophy and so serious about his planned leadership bid that he has unleashed North America's second-oldest crewcut (only Mickey Spillane's has lasted longer) and let it grow out, a severe blow to ww Two nostalgia buffs.

There are others, too droll or dull to mention. To represent the three Western provinces, Trudeau has had to dip into the Senate for a puzzling collection of talent. Saskatchewan's representative, Hazen Argue, is a turncoat, who was an ambitious socialist until he was beaten by Tommy Douglas for leader of the New Democratic Party. He jumped to the Liberals in 1961 and when he was appointed to the Senate in 1966, David Lewis rose in the Commons and said, "We have made progress in our civilization. The thirty pieces of silver have now become half a million dollars, which is what Mr. Argue has been paid for being what he was." At forty-five, Argue had a safe thirty years to go in the Senate until mandatory retirement at a then annual wage of $15,000, which would have been worth $450,000. He has since been rewarded three-fold.

The representative from Alberta is another turncoat, Bud Olson, who was a Social Credit MP until induced to become a

Liberal and received the usual Senate reward when he was defeated, as all Liberals in these three provinces are.

British Columbia is represented in the cabinet by two men who represent no voter. One, Jack Austin, is a former defeated Liberal candidate. He is an artful dodger with a brilliant mind, a lawyer who turned mining promoter in the bucket-shop days of the Vancouver Stock Exchange. While a mining promoter, he mysteriously became a Queen's Counsel four days before going to Ottawa — arranged with Premier W.A.C. Bennett by Austin's old friend Paul Martin, whom he supported at the 1968 Liberal leadership convention.

Austin lasted just fifteen months as Trudeau's principal secretary before accusations about his past appeared in the press and threatened questions in the Commons by the Tories, speeding his elevation to the Senate. He was just forty-three at the time, and the payoff stretching the thirty-two years until he is seventy-five will total $937,600 — an improvement on Argue's reward.

The second B.C. minister is a well-meaning throwback, a stentorian wheelhorse named Ray Perrault who is known as either Senator Phogbound or, in Victoria, Phineas T. Windbag. Thrown out of work by the voters, and before his Senate reward came through, Perrault was fixed with an amorphous job with Jack Davis (then a Trudeau minister before being defeated, turning Social Credit and being sacked from the B.C. cabinet for turning his first-class air tickets in for economy seats and pocketing the difference). Enraged by the anti-Trudeaucrat stand taken on CBC Vancouver by commentator Ben Metcalfe, Perrault recorded the critical comments on his own tape recorder and Davis actually raised the issue in the Commons, demanding that this treasonous soul be sacked by the CBC. Mr. Metcalfe no longer appears on the CBC.

A man with a fuse the length of a cigarette butt, Perrault responded thusly to a Vancouver hot-line caller who disagreed with him: "You strike me as not very intelligent, a drag on society." The next woman caller: "Well, I guess I'm just another drag on society." Perrault, who at the time was government leader in the Senate: "Don't phone up here and abuse politicians."

Sometimes you don't have to; they do it to themselves. Perrault, in full flight, often strangles on his own convoluted verbiage and pageboys must be summoned to disentangle him from his syntax before it cuts off his air supply. He is such a shameless partisan that, when he was in the Commons, the word was that he wore out two desk tops per session, his enthusiastic thumping at his leader's eloquence so physical that it reduced the desk top to kindling.

The casual way Trudeau approaches the cabinet, its selection and nurturing is illustrated by the consumer and corporate affairs ministry. You could make a case that under the Liberals, pig owners may be better represented in Canada than consumers. The *Directory of Associations* lists seven associations under "Consumer Protection," fifteen under "Swine."

The record of Pierre "Just Society" Trudeau in the struggle between consumers and the business world is a joke. Canada still has the weakest anticombines legislation of any so-called civilized country. Trudeau has used the portfolio as a neglected way station, shuffling ministers through in revolving-door fashion. A look at the record indicates the PM's lack of interest in having an effective watchdog on consumer and corporate interests.

When Ron Basford succeeded John Turner in the early Trudeau years, he introduced Bill C-256, the Competition Act. The *London Sunday Times* called it "the most sweeping antitrust legislation in North American history." That was 1971. A furious and heavily financed lobby from business interests — Basford was called "a dangerous fanatic" — achieved its aim. The bill was killed, Basford was dropped from the ministry in early 1972 and his senior mandarins removed.

In his place, Trudeau planted the compliant Andras, a Lakehead auto dealer who, applauded *The Canadian Grocer*, had "the entrepreneurial wisdom of a successful salesman." Andras, cochairman of the upcoming 1972 election campaign, knew that Liberal bagmen had found slim pickings among infuriated businessmen — a large factor, as it turned out, in the Grits being subsequently dumped into a minority situation. He announced that a revised competition bill would be reintroduced.

After the election, Herb Gray became minister. By April 1974, he had a bill to amend the Combines Investigation Act. The day he opened debate, the Liberal frontbenches were empty. The next month, an election was called and he was dumped from the cabinet. André Ouellet, who succeeded him, had to resign by 1976 when he made some understandable (if inflamed) comments about a judge after Canada's major sugar companies were acquitted in an antitrust case.

Bryce Mackasey was then in and out of the portfolio so fast the revolving door didn't even have time to cool his temper.

The Trudeau genius then appointed Tony Abbott, the genial lightweight who had spent all his previous incarnation in an anticonsumer mode. Son of a former Liberal finance minister, he was executive assistant to that quintessential corporate figure, Robert Winters, and followed him to Brascan, where he was corporate counsel to the food and brewing concerns of the conglomerate.

Next, apprenticing as a champion of consumers, Abbott was president of the Retail Council of Canada, a lobby for the chain stores. In one impassioned speech, he referred to "Comrade Ron" Basford and "Commissar David" — a reference to the respected David Henry, director of investigations and research in the ministry Abbott later was to head. *Beautiful!* Tony Abbott, a flack for corporate interests, is Trudeau's choice as the defender of the consumer.

After little more than a year, Abbott was shuffled to the small business portfolio where he belonged. In came Warren Allmand, a burned-out case after being lied to by the barn-burning Mounties when solicitor-general. And now — you'll never guess. We have the recycled André Ouellet, contrite and cautious, back where he started out.

Just as bad was the treatment of the senior staff. Once it was obvious the Trudeaucrats were backing away from the original Competition Act, Henry resigned to go to the Supreme Court of Ontario. Once it was clear the Liberals would allow

Bill C-256 to die on the order paper, deputy minister Jim Grandy left.

In his first ten years in office, the idealist author of The Just Society had seven different ministers and six deputy ministers waft their way through the portfolio. He is now working on his ninth appointment in thirteen years. Does he care? We'll leave it to you.

In toto, Mr. Trudeau has expanded his cabinet to thirty-six bodies, the highest number in Canadian history. It means one-quarter of the entire Liberal caucus, with a majority government, is now in the cabinet. It means that the Trudeaucrat cabinet is now larger than the entire legislature of Prince Edward Island.

It is a cabinet without spark, without wit, without any real oratorical skills, save the now-discredited MacEachen and a Trudeau who less and less often rouses himself. He seldom addresses the House of Commons he disdains in a full speech more than two or three times a year and so debases the coinage. He is a bored man and we are the recipients of his boredom.

It is a cabinet not trusted by the Opposition parties and not respected by the public It is a testimony to Pierre Trudeau as a leader and selector of what are deemed to be his most talented followers.

5
Second Stopover

Ottawa Revisited
with a Vengeance

Hot air and cold warfare . . .
the symbiotic suckling of politicians,
press and swivel servants . . .
mouths stuffed with bafflegab, minds
filled with persiflage . . .
Ennui-on-the-Rideau

Ottawa, Yesterday's City Tomorrow, is at the base of our ills. "Queen Victoria's Mistake," as the city is fondly known, is the coldest capital city in the world next to Ulan Bator. As Casey Stengel used to say, you can look it up.

If Winnipeg's climate can be described as ten months winter and two months hard sledding, Ottawa is best defined as Earmuff and Armpit City. When one isn't in use, the other is. God in Her wisdom, when She invented us, did not really intend human beings to spend their lives in spots with *two* bad seasons. Canadians must suffer because their capital, by error, was planted in a spot that alternates mosquito dive-bombers with Arctic blizzards and the denizens — naturally — wish to share their misery with the rest of their fellow citizens. It is called co-operative federalism.

The residents of Ottawa maintain that bundling up in seven layers of clothing before venturing to the corner Mac's Milk for a pound of prefrozen butter builds character and improves the breed.

It doesn't. It just makes you surly.

Anyone who must shovel his way down the steps, chip the ice from his car, hold a match to the door lock to thaw it and then inch to work behind a snow plow is not going to smile at his desk — he is going to take revenge on his fellow Canadians by venting his spleen on the people in happier circumstances.

Lots of people in Saskatchewan and Newfoundland endure the same day's beginnings, but they have worthwhile work ahead. As the man once said, at any university, the top third of the class goes on to become professors, the second third goes to work for government, and the other third has to go out and earn a living. A bemused outsider, as your faithful agent is, is continually struck by the number of Ottawa residents who actually *think* they lead a normal existence, that this beehive of self-stroking represents reality.

In essence, this is its major sin: it is an artificial city, as artificial as any company town built around a pulp mill on an isolated B.C. inlet. Tennessee Ernie Ford's line, *I owe my soul to the company store*, though he didn't know it, was written for Ottawa. All three species that populate the town — the politicians, the press and the swivel servants — suck off the same giant teat, Mother Government.

There is a natural ambience, a symbiotic relationship (though superficial antagonisms remain, rather like Jack Benny-Fred Allen feuds) since there is a shared experience that is mated, in essence, to a mutual good. Knocking the product, it is felt, is knocking everyone's pay cheque. Ottawa is rather like Detroit: those who dump on this year's model of tin are thought of, in truth, as having a small essence of treason in their souls.

I argue about this with my friends and journalistic colleagues, Charles Lynch and Doug Fisher, settled inhabitants and chroniclers of the upper-middle-class capital of the world. *Of course* it's a comfortable town for those who wish to spend the rest of their lives there, cosseted by the parks, theatres, skating canals and bicycle paths paid for by the unwashed of Moncton and Kamloops. That's the point — why it is such an unreal, artificial place for the dispensing of governmental wisdom. The residents have a vested reason (the journalists included) for maintaining Ottawa's privileged anthill, prepared even to endure the loathsome climate so as to be members of what, perforce, is an exclusive club: i.e., excluding *all* Canadians not privy to the perks.

74

It is Canada's own Brasilia, its own Canberra, artificially created enclaves, hermetically sealed from the realities that a politician getting on the subway or trying to hail a taxi in London, Paris or even Washington, must endure. In Ottawa, one bicycles, mentally as well as physically. There are designated paths for both. One never freelances.

There have been transplants to Ennui-on-the-Rideau who have been around for years, still wandering around in a daze, their minds stuffed with bafflegab and their mouths filled with persiflage — and vice versa. The first rule that must be remembered is that Rockcliffe matrons, who run the town, speak only to cabinet ministers, who speak only to Pierre Trudeau, who speaks only to God or himself — whichever comes first to mind. I was once at a black-tied dinner of men of staggering intellect, which someone described as the greatest meeting of minds since Pierre Trudeau dined alone.

But I digress. It is impossible to buy a tank of gas in Ottawa after dark. I have encountered towns where they roll up the sidewalks at sundown (a wise man advised that you should never order a martini in a town that still has a high school band — and Ottawa still qualifies) but the capital puzzles in that it assumes no one *drives* after dark. There may be a message there. The gas jockeys of the town, emulating the swivel servants, rush home, when the sun hits the deck, to watch reruns of Desi and Lucy, the most intellectual thing to hit town since they began to show the recreations of Mackenzie King's seances.

(There is a certain justice of the Supreme Court of Canada who, noting the law of the land stipulates that Supreme Court judges must reside within forty miles of Ottawa, says that is his own personal definition of "capital punishment.")

The prime architectural boast is the Château Laurier, which looks as if it were designed by a group of Walt Disney animators who got stoned one night on strange mushrooms. The bellhops are so old they are mistaken for senior citizens and are often helped onto elevators by little old ladies. The CBC has its local radio headquarters in the loft, proving that there are indeed bats in the belfry.

The uniqueness of the cuisine of the town has to do with

the arrival — on any important feast day or national holiday — of a fleet of "chip wagons" that descend from the Quebec hills and other unknown depths of the boondocks. These are broken-down buses, looking as if they should be in the graveyards where elephants go to die, with the sides blow-torched out of them, dispensing hot french fries to otherwise deprived gourmands of the capital.

It has not yet been proven that the quality of thought coming out of Ottawa is directly related to the amount of greasy chips that are consumed, winter and summer, man and child, but it is understood that a Carleton University professor is researching a paper on it. He has received a government grant and hopes to be finished, with graduate student help, by 1986.

The locals boast grandly about the Gatineau Hills across the Ottawa River in Quebec. These are mildly undulating mounds of earth that would elsewhere be classified as topographical bumps. The local avid skiers can descend them at approximately 12.5 mph for up to 200 yards, and it is considered a great thrill. Any town raised on the oratorical delights of Mackenzie King and Allan MacEachen is easily thrilled.

One does not want to paint too truthful a picture, but truth must be observed. Ottawans think hot-tubs are located in bathrooms. Condominiums are thought to be a New Brunswick birth control device.

It is the only city in the world where rush hour starts at 3:30, the indexed-pension people fleeing the office early to hit Desi and Lucy. Men wear three-piece blue suits in July. Mandarins wear six-piece minds all year round. The Canadian flag on the Peace Tower goes up and down like a toilet seat as senators die off.

Ottawa (bland on the outside, comatose on the inside) has all the verve of a glass of champagne that has been left standing for two days. I have two favourite vignettes. Sparks Street, the former main drag of this swamp town, has been turned into a pedestrian mall in vain hopes of injecting some humanity into what is basically and irrevocably an inhumane ambience. Scattered sculptures and fainthearted fountains speckle this attempt at pseudo-Rome, and the idea is that a casual, free-flow of pedestrian traffic through what could be a brick Omaha will transfuse a touch of joy into a purse-lipped city.

At each narrow cross street there is a traffic light — designed for the *cars*. But the pedestrians — *Ottawa* pedestrians, conditioned to *obey* — stand dutifully, watching absentmindedly the usually empty two lanes of traffic and refuse to travel the further twelve steps of their casual stroll until the unrelenting red light (their master, their guide, their Ottawa mind-gauge) tells them it's okay to proceed.

Only in Germany have I seen such blind, unblinking obedience at the street level. It is not learned. It is *conditioned*. Ottawa has ways to make you conform.

The second delightful indicator is the elevator of the Booth Building, 165 Sparks Street. It leads to the National Press Club and a vast clutch of the Ottawa offices of important newspapers, magazines and radio networks. It being Ottawa-run, the numbers on the elevator buttons keep falling off. The repairmen, being Ottawa-run, have lazily patched things up: the "odd" panel reads "1-3-4-6" and the "even" panel, "2-3-5-8."

Strangers enter the elevator, puzzle, and ride up and down for ten minutes searching for their destinations. Little old ladies break out in tears. A sometimes resident of an office up the street, I have watched this tableau with interest for more than a year. The botched-up buttons remain and no one — the tough journalist tenants upstairs who overthrow governments and destroy cabinet ministers — complains. It's accepted. This is Ottawa. You can't get there from here.

You still cannot fly directly from the capital of the country, in the year of Her Lord 1982, to New York on the People's Airline. The only nonstop flight to that regular destination of high snivel servants and other grateful escapees is a recent experiment by the U.S.-owned Pilgrim Airlines, with headquarters in the metropolis of New London, Connecticut, a delightful adventure in Captain Eddy Ricketyback flying. The craft is a two-engine forty-four-seat Fokker, which always gives the impression it is about to land in a jungle clearing to pick up a cache of marijuana. A colleague went aboard with carry-on luggage — and they *lost* it. However, it does get you to New York on one hop, which the People's Airline, run by the People's Government, cannot do eighty-nine years after the Wright Brothers. You still cannot fly from the capital of Canada to the capital of the United States. Complicated arrangements take you through Toronto or Montreal or Baltimore (from Baltimore you make your way by bus). Ottawa is Canada's own Transylvania, a hidden destination off the byways of the nation. It is the Rodney Dangerfield of Canadian cities, never getting any respect because it shies from normal connecting routes. What should be the centrepiece of the country is a wallflower.

The miasma hits at the Ottawa airport, a one-horse structure befitting Medicine Hat, but not the national capital. A plunge into the terminal is a plunge into a sea of briefcases filled with despair, of weekend faces without joy, end-of-day visages abrim to the jowls with the burden of no laughter. A backwater assigned the responsibility of feeling more important than it really is, Ottawa takes itself very seriously. You can tell the permanent residents by the white Plimsoll line on the lower shin line of their trousers, testimony to the salt in the gutter that destroys all automobile fenders, laps over the overshoes and marks a mandarin for life.

There is a significant message in the newsstand — crowded, disorganized and littered with magazines arriving two days after the rest of Canada gets them. The daily papers are cleverly placed at knee-height under an overhanging ledge. To find the name of the paper wanted, one must almost get down on all fours. It is symbolic, educational: to get any information in Ottawa, one must first kneel. It is a most salutory introduction to the town.

Your ink-stained wretch, when he is not spending his time on airplanes, spends it in airport taxis. I am Canada's leading expert on taxis. I am here to say that Ottawa's taxis, for reasons that escape me, are the dirtiest, smelliest, most slovenly taxis in the country.

The Ottawa terminal, shrewdly designed by the same people who run the country, is structured — in this small

78

town — so that one must wrestle one's bag further than in Montreal, Toronto, Vancouver, Winnipeg or elsewhere. There are no luggage carts. Ottawa has yet to discover them.

The taxi lineup has all the discipline of a Chinese fire drill. Montreal cabbies are talkative. In Toronto, they are swift and distracted. In Vancouver, they are likely to be Ph.D.'s in Chaucerian poetry who spend their days at the nude Wreck Beach. In Ottawa? Just surly. I have encountered more surly Ottawa taxi drivers than I have surly politicians in the Liberal cabinet, where I have many friends and admirers.

When the foot-well in the back seat is not full of melted snow (riding in an Ottawa taxi in the winter, I know for the first time how a woman feels in the stirrups), it is full of last week's soggy newspapers. When the lining of the car is not redolent of this day's Col. Sanders, it is reminiscent of terminal sweat-sock. Those high people in charge of such things as our airport taxis and our nostrils are unaware of these boring details of ordinary life, as their ministerial limos meeting them at the airport are sprayed twice daily with the afterbreath of an executive assistant. (If they ever banned gin in this town, the political machinery would dry up like the transmission in a 1932 Hupmobile.)

Coma City, Pavlov's secret retreat, has a delightful tableau in summer on the Sparks Street mall, as the swivel servants — drugstore cowboys on high salaries — stand about in their white shoes, glomming the stenographers. (There are a number of them in what we call the Full Winnipeg — white shoes, white belt, white tie.)

Layabouts from the Ottawa Valley, their tick-ridden long locks indicating they have not been informed that the 1960s have ended, pick plaintively at their guitars, their empty-of-dimes cases in front of them, indicating their talents. Government employees stand enraptured at the noon hour, their daily struggle with seniority suspended for one thin sarsaparilla, listening to a free Dixieland band playing on the mall. The subsidy comes not from city hall, but Amnesty International.

There is a suspended animation syndrome to the place. Couriers hand-deliver copies of cabinet ministers' speeches that were delivered a week previously in Moncton or Moosomin. Air Canada delivers tickets, reserved four days previously, in an envelope marked RUSH! Government flacks at garden parties wear three-piece suits of bulletproof wool, their flinty eyes aimed more at promotion than perspiration. It is a town in a constant sweat of anticipation — tenure the goal, pension the heaven. Recession-proof, it is a town that walks in molasses.

Ottawa is a town masquerading as a city, filled with paper and topped with gas. In 1905 Henry James toured Philadelphia and found that on Sunday mornings its boulevards were "vacant of everything but an immeasurable bourgeois blankness." That is Ottawa midweek. Another Philadelphia visitor in the same era was Lincoln Steffens, the famed muckraker, who found it "corrupt and contented." That is Ottawa, corrupt in its conceit, contented because it knows not what it is. A 1905 Philadelphia: not a bad definition of 1982 Ottawa.

People who persist in Ottawa are people who, when you get down to it, enjoy being punished, changing shirts three times daily in the sauna that passes for summer, frigid midgets with rigid digits in the winter, revelling in their suffering. The Marquis de Sade could have had a lot to say about this town — and could possibly expand upon its peculiarities.

The fix the country is in can be explained a lot by the fact that the people who run it, all denizens of this burg, secretly enjoy existing in such punishing sterility and, by transference, wish to pass on the suffering to those out in the boondocks who are deprived of Ottawa's salubrious masochism.

The country needs a shrink more than it needs a prime minister.

6
Second
Digression

The Bachelor Party

Mackenzie King as kinky little prototype...
Trudeau as the lifetime loner
who dabbled in marriage...
MacEachen as the link who missed...
wee Jimmy Coutts as the sotto voce
bachelor apparent

There is something strange about Canada. It is the home of The Bachelor Party. It enjoys being run by lonely, selfish men — that being one definition of a bachelor. Does this mean our leaders (Ottawa? the country?) don't like sex? Or does it mean that our leaders (Ottawa? the country?) are promiscuous? A discussion follows.

William Lyon Mackenzie King, that kinky little cutey, ran this nation for twenty-two years in three different spells, 1921 to 1926, a pause, 1926 to 1930, 1935 to 1948. We just kept coming back for more punishment.

Pierre Trudeau, on examination, is a lifetime bachelor who dabbled absentmindedly in marriage for a brief five years with the lovely Margaret and now seems quite the most self-contained single parent in the universe. He lived quite contentedly until he was fifty-one as a bachelor and now, at sixty-three, seems quite contented again.

Bachelorhood seems to be his natural state, the married spasm an aberration. In her first book, *Beyond Reason*, Margaret revealed that he once told her the thing he liked best about his mother was that she never disturbed him. Ah, there lies a true bachelor. There lies a natural leader for Canada, the country that is so polite it never disturbs the saintly reveries of the guru who is so charitable as to lead us.

Here is the key to Canada's survival as a country that boasts no revolutions, brooks no assassinations, spurns class warfare and puts all of its money into savings accounts. For over half of the past sixty years it has been run by bachelors who, if they liked women, showed it in a very peculiar way.

When you examine this turgid country closely, you will find the secret is that it *enjoys* being ruled by lonely, austere bachelors. If the essence, the personality of a country can be judged by the verve of a John Kennedy or the growling lion of a Churchill, Canada is best epitomized by grim, abstemious bachelors pulling the shawls around their feet on February eves.

It fits, therefore, that the game plan of The Bachelor Party, before his hand calculator misfired, was for the second leading bachelor of Ottawa, Allan J. MacEachen, to succeed to the mantle of leadership. At 61, he had well proved his credentials for the job (i.e., avoiding the altar).

Alas, his budget fumblitis killed those chances but The Bachelor Party, always with good bench strength, had a man in reserve. He was wee Jimmy Coutts, who seems to have the *sotto voce* approval of the Big Bachelor himself and certainly has the backing of Senator Keith Davey, The Rainmaker who dispenses dew on the heads of all Grit princes.

Coutts, renowned a bit as a ladies' man and a coveted catch at the right dinner parties, has a good head start on the required credentials by remaining, at forty-four, unsullied and unhitched. He has only to gaze at the leadership of those before him. He hasn't far to go.

Mackenzie King kept on friendly relations with a succession of happily married women, while doing his nighttime missionary projects with prostitutes. (There's the old Ottawa joke about King ending cabinet sessions: "Meeting adjourned. Could any of you fellows lend me ten bucks?")

Trudeau likes young women; so many of his Ottawa dates have an uncanny resemblance to (and are approximately the same age as) Margaret.

Like King, MacEachen's friendships with women tend to be with happily married wives or widows. They're safe. His best friends are Trudeau aide Joyce Fairbairn (Mrs. Michael

Gillan; Gillan works for MacEachen) and his personal secretary, Pearl Hunter, a widow who was once secretary to Jimmy Sinclair, Margaret's father.

MacEachen's male friends are mostly bachelors: Alistair Fraser, former clerk of the Commons; John Stewart, the former MP from Antigonish; the priests at St. Francis Xavier University who first boosted him. He goes to mass almost every day. There is a natural link between the brooding Presbyterian King — separated by the pseudo-swinging Trudeau — and the brooding Catholic MacEachen.

It is understandable that Ottawa is a bachelor haven, despite the four to one ratio of females to males in government service. It is a town composed of men who need a committee before they can make a decision. Once home, they are lost without a third party to break the tie. They need a quorum, and that tends to get crowded in the kitchen.

Ottawa, essentially, is a coitus interruptus town. Any place where decisions are two parts delay to one part deny is, perforce, a bad bet in the sheets. It's understandable. Margaret complained in her second book about how Pierre shipped her to a separate bedroom in the attic. That's no surprise. That's a metaphor for what the party has been doing to the rest of the country for years.

Toronto sociologist Dr. Edward Shorter, in a *Saturday Night* piece examining Ottawa's sensuousness, wrote about the way the sexual tension crackled on Friday night around the Press Club bar. The suspicion is that he was listening to the pretzels.

Ottawa, when you get down to it, is the civic equivalent of saltpetre. Only the pensions are indexed; very little else goes up on a regular basis. It's the nature of the place, spontaneity frowned upon and joy severely taxed. A city that lives at the Xerox machine eventually has to suffer some internal damage — mainly a curvature of the imagination.

One of the many disappointments of the Trudeau era is that the expected flowering of the arts and the finer things, anticipated when Camelot North sprung forth from a trampoline, never happened. The home of the rich intellectual, expected to become sort of an Athens-of-the-Arctic, did not materialize. Neither did the city's artistic establishment. Under Trudeau, the capital's national galleries and museums have never been in worse shape.

Sondra Gotlieb, author and wife of Allan Gotlieb, Canadian ambassador to Washington, traces the descent into ennui to the departure of a bundle of lively political wives who fled with their husbands once it was apparent the PM in fact did not intend to reinvent an artistic Nineveh by the Ottawa River: Ruth Macdonald, Geills Turner, Valerie Gibson, Adrian Lang, Jane Faulkner and others of that disappointed era. Just as the tone of any party is set by the mood of the hostess, the tone of Ottawa is determined by the dominant ministerial wives. It is not for nothing that the home of the prime minister is known as 24 Nosex Drive.

Mackenzie King tried to commune with his dead mother and talked to his beloved dog. MacEachen talks to his broken calculator, and Coutts talks to Davey who talks only to Goldfarb. Trudeau (the famous nonnewspaper reader) revealed during the 1981 CBC technicians' strike that it wasn't important because he never listened to radio or watched TV. It is natural. The voters of this country like monks, inward-turning men who are obsessed with self.

It is not an accident that Liberal leaders are bachelors and bachelors are Liberals. It goes with the territory.

7
Ontario
*The Complacency Capital
of the World*

Buttermilk Billy and the Regressive
Conservatives . . . depravity on the silver screen . . .
fag-bashings as election sport . . .
hanging up on the Francophones . . .
a place to withstand

One evening several years ago Dr. Stuart Smith, then the Ontario Liberal leader, delivered a searing, ad lib message from the heart to a collection of fellow Liberals in the basement of a motor hotel in suburban Winnipeg. It was one of those "workshops" — the political buzzword for hair-pulling sessions — and Smith, growing heated, had just dazzled the room with the fever of his feelings on the party's problems.

I upped to him later and said, in admiration, that if he talked like that at home he would be premier of Ontario.

He snorted at my ignorance. "If I talked like that at home," he said, "I'd lose my own seat." A psychiatrist from Montreal who got into Ontario politics via his practice in Hamilton, Smith explained that he had been years in Ontario before he finally realized there are different definitions of the word passionate.

As someone raised in Quebec, he had always thought to be "passionate" was a compliment — a person who felt strongly, who was eager and determined. In Ontario, he found to his eventual sorrow, a "passionate" individual was regarded as slightly unbalanced, demented if not deranged.

"I've only just learned this," he sighed. "And *I'm* a psychiatrist."

All of this explains why Brampton Bill Davis, so dull you can slice it, rules Ontario with a comfortable majority and why Dr. Stuart Smith, suppressed passionate idealist, is now out of politics, having blunted his sword against the forehead of the turgid Ontario voter. If you want to understand Ontario, you must remind yourself that the Regressive Conservative party has now been in power longer than any regime in the universe with the lone exception that comes to mind: Moscow. It is the longest-running political show in what is amusingly called the free world.

In 1943, when the Tories of Ontario began their string, Joe Louis was in his prime. Hitler was still around and kicking. Franklin Delano Roosevelt and Mackenzie King consumed the front pages. Children didn't talk back. Grass was something you mowed.

Bulgaria has not had a government that has lasted as long. Nor Albania or Romania — other bastions of democracy. Even Alberta changes masters more often. Only Ontario, of all the Canadian provinces, remains content with a mandate that will run forty-two years before another election is necessary. There is an electorate of consummate contentment.

Ontario is probably the complacency capital of the world. Cosseted by a 115-year-old policy that deemed the rest of Canada a hinterland for the benefit of Ontario industry, the residents naturally reward their benefactors. The Tories of Buttermilk Bill and predecessors have been in power for twelve straight terms. They have done this by appealing to the most conservative people in Canada, the comfortable burghers of southern Ontario.

To keep these burghers happy, Bill Davis ensured that for five years sophisticated Toronto was the only city in major league baseball where you were not allowed a cardboard cup of beer. (The pinch-faced ban was finally lifted this summer and, at last report, no crazed fans went berserk in the streets, intent on pillage.) To keep these burghers happy, Davis allows his censors to ban *The Tin Drum*, a film that won the Palme d'or at the Cannes Film Festival and an Oscar at the Academy Awards.

Caligula has been running in Vancouver for fifty-five weeks. The residents of the largest and richest and allegedly most advanced city in the country, Toronto, are not allowed to see it, since it would corrupt and deprave them. Ontario has a film censorship policy that would fit well in P.E.I., because Buttermilk Bill is not looking at Toronto, he's looking at the burghers of southern Ontario. Brampton asserts its morals on Bloor Street.

To keep these burghers happy, Davis was prepared to play on the anti-French vote so as to win the majority that escaped him in two previous elections.

Section 133 of the British North America Act (imaginatively retitled the Constitution Act 1867) is the one that gives status to both French and English in the courts and legislature of Quebec. Manitoba, with its small French-speaking population, has been instructed by the courts to honour Section 133. Richard Hatfield's New Brunswick, with its Acadian segment, has voluntarily invoked Section 133.

The Ontario of Bill Davis, with the largest French-speaking community outside Quebec, has stubbornly resisted accepting into law the essential that binds this bilingual country together — acceptance of the fact that a Francophone resident of Ontario has a right (as does an Anglophone resident of Quebec) to a trial in his own language.

Bill Davis, that pink-cheeked, pipe-smoking exemplar of Brampton church-going, is the most expedient politician in Canada. Peter Lougheed is single-minded to the point of inflexibility. Pierre Trudeau is a prisoner of his own ego. René Lévesque is obsessed with giving his own people equality with the lordly Anglos. But Bill Davis, smiling Bill Davis, is superior to all of them in his religiosity, his worshipping before the shrine of power — and what he will do to retain it. What he will do is not pleasant.

To remain top of the heap, Ontario's supposedly solid leaders resorted to trading tricks like a cut-rate streetwalker. It was Davis who was largely responsible for the scuppering of the only Tory government to appear on the federal scene since Jack Pickersgill was a pup. Because Joe Clark, in his fumbling honesty, was prepared to pay Alberta close to fair value for its oil, the Davis government withdrew the awesome slickness of the Big Blue Machine. Davis himself, for his contribution to the 1980 Clark defeat, retreated to the wisdom of his Florida condominium for practically all the campaign.

To remain at what they think is top of the heap, Davis and his Tories willingly deserted the Tory premiers of Alberta, Manitoba, Nova Scotia, Prince Edward Island and Newfoundland by leaping into bed with Pierre Trudeau and his arrogant unilateral stance on the constitution.

In return, of course, for Trudeau's support for the Davis position that Ontario — alone of all its manufacturing competitors in the U.S. and abroad — did not have to pay even close to the world price for the oil it received from Alberta. Protected Ontario industry, which supplies Bill Davis' party funds, refuses to pay the price for oil that its international competitors must pay. So Bill Davis supports Liberal Trudeau in the fight with Tory Lougheed — meanwhile sinking Tory Clark in the election.

In return, also, for the Trudeau blind eye to the fact that Ontario will not give its five hundred thousand Francophones the same equality under the law that Quebec gives its Anglophones. There are ninety-five thousand children in Ontario attending French schools. In a high school in Hamilton, French-language students say they are afraid to speak French in the corridors because they were forever being called "frogs." Bill Davis knows this. So he refuses to accept Section 133.

In return, Ottawa's Liberal-controlled constitutional committee approved — during Davis' 1981 election campaign — a resolution allowing Ontario to wriggle out of Section 133 guarantees. So Pierre Trudeau, who fought valiantly against René Lévesque's Bill 101 — insisting that Quebec's Anglophone minority retain its rights — refuses to insist that Bill Davis grant the same rights to his Francophone minority.

It is wheel and deal with principles. It is political Wintario. Bill Davis knows he has the last of the Orange Lodge bigots. Ontario is one of the last places where they still have King Billy parades on 12 July.

(Not a single civil libertarian voice was raised in Ottawa, it should be added, when Toronto police, in crowbar-swinging glee, raided four homosexual bathhouses and hauled in the biggest mass arrest since Trudeau's War Measures Act — a week after Davis had called his election. Fag-bashing is very popular in rural Ontario, coincidentally at election time.)

It's hard to believe, but the Grand Orange Lodge, which came to Canada during the Protestant-Catholic tension in Ireland with a rallying cry of One Flag, One Country and One Language, still has a march through downtown Toronto as King Billy rides his white horse to celebrate the Glorious Twelfth.

King Billy doesn't count that much anymore, but the thought of him still does in the mind of Premier Billy, master manipulator of the shadows of puritanism and antipopery.

To save himself on the constitution, Trudeau went into the alliance with the Tories of Queen's Park and thus put in peril yet another provincial Liberal party. Both Dr. Smith, who left in despair to head the Science Council of Canada, and new leader David Peterson attempted to distance themselves from their superiors in Ottawa, a link to Trudeau being seen as death at the polling booth.

Ontario at the moment is confused, the locus of Toronto dominating the country but the province as a whole reeling from its unaccustomed relegation into the realm of economic trouble. Bad times were always associated with those whiners in the hinterland. Under Bill Davis, the province has lost the prestige it enjoyed under John Robarts as the linchpin of Confederation connected to Quebec.

That respect has gone and now its economic domination is threatened. It will never be in need of humility pills, but Ontario these days is pondering its future a bit. Any pause for contemplation is greatly appreciated — and watched from afar with small amusement.

8
Third Stopover

Toronto
The Big Lemon

Municipal penis envy . . .
pecuniary mea culpa . . .
S and M at Exhibition Stadium . . .
astronomy of the Sun, *the* Star *and the* Globe . . .
Trudeau and the media daisy chain

*J*ust as New York is an entity unto itself, divorced from the rest of America, Toronto is a thing apart, revelling in its chauvinism. It is no more connected with Canada than London is with the Cotswolds, or the moors of Yorkshire, or the downs of Kent. Just as Paris is a world to itself, alien to its rural cousins.

Toronto and the Ontario of Buttermilk Billy are entirely separate. (This is why B.B. has his chauffeur drive him home the twenty-five miles to Brampton most every night; he does not wish to be contaminated by the ambience of a foreign culture.)

The problem with Toronto is that it is imitative. It does not want to be itself. The Big Lemon (as it is known in Western Canada) suffers from municipal penis envy. In shooting through its pubescent era, from the pinch-faced Presbyterian enclave into a fern-bar and Perrier pitstop, it always had role models. New York was its ideal; it also wanted San Francisco's restaurants and Vancouver's clean streets, Atlanta's affluence and Peterborough's rectitude.

That never works. Jealousy is always self-destructive. Toronto, instead, is a failed Boston in that it is always looking over its shoulder, afeared that someone may be gaining. There is a compulsion to create a society on someone else's model.

The greatest civic boast is an erection in the sky that beat out a guywire-supported tower in Poland for the record book. This is accomplishment? The Metro Toronto chairman, Paul Godfrey, has a perm and a jawlift; he succeeds in looking like nothing so much as a superannuated teen-ager in gold chains. Bob Guccione comes to the council table.

There is a reason why the only city in Canada to have its own town fool — Harold Ballard — has also the worst teams in sport, the Argonauts, the Maple Leafs, the Blue Jays, the Blizzard. Toronto, one must understand, has no collective psyche, no real reason for being other than as a collection plate and siphoning pan for money created elsewhere.

The supposedly failing city of Montreal consistently produces baseball and hockey clubs (and occasionally football teams when shell-game artists from Vancouver are not involved) that are models of good management, pride and performance.

Toronto, in the meantime, has managed to capture a monopoly on the most dreadful collection of spavined hacks and ill-coordinated gorillas ever assembled — all representing this brave new pile of money that is held up as the new Periclean Athens.

The Argos secretly kept the country united in shared laughter at their ineptness. The once-mighty Leafs, the goal of every Canadian boy with Eaton's catalogues for shin pads, are now a comic staple. The Blue Jays are baseball's answer to paint-by-number. The money-losing Toronto Blizzard pro soccer team — as inept as their choice of name — completes as stunningly incompetent a clutch of stumblebums as ever represented one city.

Those grim masochists who sit in the CNE grandstand, game after game in great numbers to watch the Argos slop around as waves of newly arrived imports, coaches and general managers mill about, tacitly enjoy the humiliation inflicted upon them by invaders from Regina, Edmonton and other unknown datelines. The Torontonian, knowing deep in his soul that he represents naught but avarice and whose cultural base is about as thin as the mustard on his niggardly hotdog, feels a need for a punishment that will be gone by Monday morning. It's an S-and-M trip but without the scars that would be embarrassing in the golf club Jacuzzi.

The Montreal sports fan goes out into the afternoon or evening proudly, aware that an extension of his being, his love of life, is going to be displayed on ice or diamond within the next few hours. He dresses for the role, flamboyantly, and eats and drinks and sings in a *celebration* of self. Those are not sweaty jocks out there — that is *Quebec*.

The Toronto fan is on a mission of expiation, prepared to pour out his guilt to the rest of the nation as if out of a four-gallon maple syrup tin. By the transmission of vibrations, this religious pecuniary *mea culpa* is inexorably injected into the pores of the poor players, who feel the waves of angst wafting down from the grandstands upon them. They swoon. The nation rejoices.

The interesting point about the Toronto of 1982 is that while it controls more of the financial levers in the country than ever before, it is less powerful politically. That is a result of Pierre Trudeau's driving away (or allowing to drift away) the strong men who, coming from the largest and most powerful city in Canada, would naturally be effective spokesmen for the two-thirds of the country that is not Francophone. This is one reason why the country has turned against Trudeau: the strong men refuse to participate in government as long as he is there.

Today mighty Toronto is represented in cabinet by five ministers so junior in rank and respect that even their mothers have trouble remembering their names. John Roberts, Jim Fleming, Paul Cosgrove, Bob Kaplan, Charles Caccia — does anyone have any illusion about how much clout they have around the cabinet table when the going gets rough and the rough get going? It is to laugh.

Ottawa is always nervous/jealous of Toronto's power. When Phil Givens, who was a very popular Toronto mayor, perceived greater roles ahead for himself and went to Ottawa in the 1968 Trudeaumania sweep, he was placed, so as to dilute his ego, in the back row, his bald pate stroking the

Commons curtains. In the early months, Givens tried so hard to get the Speaker's attention, flexing his knees in anticipation so often only to be ignored, that he developed the bends. He gave up in disgust and retreated to Toronto.

When Joe Clark, the hiccup of history, came to power for a brief dull moment in 1979, he was presented with possibly the most popular mayor in Toronto's history, David Crombie, the hero of Rosedale after vanquishing the Grit white hope Dr. John Evans, the former University of Toronto president who was billed as leadership potential. Crombie, as ex-boss of the largest city in the country, had the largest budget of anyone in cabinet as health minister — yet the nervous Clark shut him out of the inner cabinet. He feared the tiny perfect one as a rival because of Crombie's street smarts and easy grace with people — two factors that Joe ain't got.

If Toronto lacks the direct political power it once had, it controls the nation's information, which today is real power. The perceptions flow from Toronto, whether on the TV networks, the excellent CBC radio (the veins of Canada), or the magazines and major newspapers. Thus, because it is insular, Toronto forces insularity on the rest of the country.

The *Toronto Star*, the largest and richest paper in the land, sent a superb reporter, Robert MacKenzie, to Quebec when the stirrings of nationalism and possible separation were apparent. Today, the *Star* has just one reporter covering the four Western provinces. There is the renowned Toronto magazine editor who discovered in recent years, to his surprise, that he was in Calgary for the first time. Magazine editors, particularly, fear to venture west of the Humber River mainly because they hesitate to voluntarily vacate the local gossip circuit — in case they might be the subjects of it.

The *Star*, although it maintains its circulation pre-eminence, is no longer the force it once was. It has strangely never been able to produce a "talk-aboutable" columnist, someone who rivetted the town's attention, since Pierre Berton and then Ron Haggart left. It is full of moral uplift and cheery features, but as a paper it is curiously humourless. The current unlikely

100

combination at the top of the newsroom management, hard-nosed Ray Timson, who is Press Club Incarnate, and Gary Lautens, the former dimpled darling of suburban housewives with his domestic turmoil column, are referred to by their reporters as "Knuckles and Chuckles."

When Alexander Ross, the former *Maclean's* managing editor and *Financial Post* columnist, went to the *Star* to write a column he made it a condition of his employment that he did not have to meet Beland Honderich, the much-feared publisher. Despite my many eons as an ink-stained wretch, I have never met Mr. Honderich, partly by design and partly by accident, and neither of us seems to have suffered grievously as a result.

The *Globe and Mail* — immortalized by columnist Richard J. Needham as the Grope and Flail, or the Mop and Pail — is going through a sticky patch at the moment, mainly due to economic conditions slicing its heavy reliance on national advertising revenue. The *Globe's* owners, the Thomson chain, accustomed to its docile nonunion empire, were clearly startled at the fierce pride of the *Globe* reporters and editors, who wore Red Guard armbands when management announced staff cuts and then took out an ad in their own paper protesting that news coverage would suffer.

The *Globe's* brave attempt to become a truly national newspaper via satellite in this geographically impossible country has proven a sometimes thing, oft-times giving the Vancouver reader less Toronto news than he would like and the Toronto reader rather more Calgary news than he would care to absorb. The proprietors must be given top marks for trying, especially since it is so far above their previous Peter Principle level.

If all else fails, there are always the celebrated "Companions Wanted" and "Toronto Introduction Services" meat markets tucked away discreetly in the *Globe's* classified ad section. They offer an astonishing insight into the modern world not examined in detail in the otherwise staid columns of the *Globe* — a reflection of wants and needs that are not advertised in the other two, supposedly lower-scale, Toronto papers.

101

Examples:

Hamilton bored housewife looking for discreet encounter with established gentleman. Box 3527, The Globe.

Afternoon delight, registered hotel guests only. Toronto 960-0572.

Attractive, mature gentleman, not into bars, enjoys serving others, seeks dominant male companion who is physically fit and capable of demanding a discreet and responsible association. Box 3485, The Globe.

A female, enquiring over the phone for curiosity's sake, is told that she can rent a male escort for a hundred dollars an hour or five hundred for the night. There are some sixty of these ads running each day. It is not known if Lord Thomson or Buttermilk Bill have heard about it yet.

Presuming Joe Clark wins the next election (one can always presume a lot about Joe and never be disappointed), a most difficult decision he avoided making was whether to put Peter Worthington in the cabinet. Compared to this, moving the embassy to Jerusalem and dismantling Petro-Canada were mere piffle.

Worthington was the bemused aspirant for the Conservative nomination in the byelection held in Broadview-Greenwood, the seat vacated by Bob Rae, who deserted Ottawa in order to take up the Ontario NDP leadership. Mr. Trudeau, detecting even through his veil of indifference the wrath of the electorate, had been reluctant to set a date for a confrontation at the polls with the voters, since they do tend to be disputatious at byelections.

For starters, Worthington would have been the first Tory minister in history to wear a large tattoo of a schooner on his left forearm. One would have paid any money to see the gapes from his colleagues the first muggy Ottawa day when the cabinet decided to get down to shirt sleeves.

Worthington's almost cult status as editor of the phenomenon known as the *Toronto Sun*, makes him such a prominent Toronto figure that he would have had to command consideration from the Clarkians, especially since they were not exactly overwhelmed with candidates for Mensa among their Toronto representatives.

The *Sun*, the most successful new paper in North America in an age when old-style newspapers are dying regularly, rose from the ashes of the *Toronto Telegram*. At first it built its success on Fleet Street's proven tabloid formula of sex, sin and soccer — known in more sedate circles as "crime, outrage and underwear."

More recently, however, it has gathered the most interesting array of columnists in any Canadian newspaper: Dalton Camp, Douglas Fisher, Worthington, William F. Buckley, Barbara Amiel, Dr. Morton Shulman, the manic Gary Dunford, Joan Sutton, John Robertson.

The old newspaper joke used to be that the *Sun*'s philosophical position ranged all the way from Worthington on the left to Lubor J. Zink on the right. Now it lurches right across into the psychological ozone of Barbara Amiel, a onetime Marxist who has gone full circle and is described by an admirer as the "best second-hand intellect in town," meaning that George Jonas, her estranged husband, has had an inordinate influence on her. Dr. Foth, as the token simp, the limp-wristed lily-livered limousine liberal, also appears on the pages, meaning that the *Sun* now carries all known colours of the political spectrum and several that haven't been invented yet.

When Peter Newman revealed in *The Acquisitors* that *Sun* publisher Doug Creighton's monthly entertainment bill for the *Sun* from Winston's, the "day-care centre for the Establishment," averaged a whopping amount, everyone in town envied Creighton and thought it a good PR investment on behalf of the paper. Creighton was outraged — apparently out of concern that his little blue-collar readers would be appalled. Instead, he should have recalled the lessons of Adam Clayton Powell, the late U.S. congressman who was never more loved by his impoverished Harlem electorate than when he splashed wads of money around some Caribbean casino. *Sun* readers like flash.

Worthington for his part, is a moralist who was a boxing

champion at university. He is also a paper millionaire, as a result of his holdings in *Sun* stock as one of the founders. His father was a general in the Canadian Army and the recent Tory aspirant fought in World War II and the Korean War. He hates communism with a passion and is contemptuous of Pierre Trudeau (whose justice minister once charged Worthington under the Official Secrets Act — thereby enhancing his martyr status among Toronto ethnics and Conservative voters). What Clark would have been able to do with him is difficult to imagine.

Worthington is a throwback to the era when newspaper editors actually had personalities and stood for something. At fifty-five, he plays softball, tries to climb Tibetan mountains, writes a ferocious column and his editorials (the *Sun* runs only one each day, enough for anyone's attention span) are unmistakable in their anger.

He seldom goes out for lunch in a town that lives on lunch gossip; he prefers to dine in his paper's cafeteria. (Newspaper lunches aren't what they used to be. They never were up to magazine lunches which, in the good days as my friend Pat Nagle recalls, were composed of "gin and mayonnaise.") But I digress.

Barbara Amiel makes a studied career of being outrageous. She polishes and perfects the role, rather as Zsa Zsa Gabor cultivates her eyelashes. Her right-wing polemics are carefully superior in tone. She is also outrageously beautiful, with a forty-one-year-old waist that would make a teenager — and does make most other women — weep.

Her personal life would fuel an entire Harlequin romance, with enough details left over for an afternoon soap. As associate editor of the *Sun*, she is newly responsible for the most feared feature in Toronto journalism, an anonymous Sunday gossip column called "Panache."

It is suitably vicious stuff, wonderfully bitchy. The column has quickly become *must* reading for the glitterati, all fearful that they might be in it.

Most people on the inside avoid Amiel because of her

104

unfortunate habit of resurrecting, for print, what were assumed to be private conversations some months or even years distant. Those she turns furious often include her own editors. While working for *Maclean's*, she was thrown into jail in Mozambique (after eating her press card in a vain attempt to avoid identification). When she volunteered the details of her adventure to *As It Happens* before *Maclean's* could get into print, *Maclean's* was not amused.

Editor Worthington was on the phone to Amiel when his secretary slipped him a note informing him that the Gouzenko family — friends of Worthington's — were on the other line. Igor Gouzenko had just died and was about to be given a secret burial. The startled Worthington passed on the news to his associate editor, who that minute was on the way to a radio broadcast, and hung up so as to get to the funeral — the only outsider invited.

Amiel proceeded to the *Andy Barrie* show on CJCL and, in her eloquence, delivered a eulogy to Gouzenko, thereby spilling Worthington's world scoop to the, um, *world*. Other radio stations, wire services, eventually the RCMP, phoned to enquire about details of the death of a man they didn't know was dead. Worthington, with a clear beat on every journalist in Canada on what should have been his personal story, was sandbagged by his own innocent associate editor. Amiel is now known around the *Sun*, from the doorman on, as "Scoop."

The point of all this is that Worthington and Amiel, who are shunned by the fashionable Toronto media mafia, are edging into acceptance in some quarters because of the extreme dislike of the lofty Trudeaucrats and the weakness of their cabinet representatives in Toronto.

The Toronto media mafia: it is many layered, multi-faceted, a species that can be dissected only by an outsider. In a fey way, one conjures up faint images — in a wild stretch of the imagination — with another daisy chain of intellectual forefrontism, the Bloomsbury group of London. Toronto is not London, and this group is not Bloomsbury, but everything is relative. (This is a digression within a digression.)

The analogy is that an interlocking band of salon partners set the tone — and the standards of those not worthy to join. As Virginia Woolf, Lytton Strachey, E. M. Forster, John Maynard Keynes *et al* established a style that depended mainly on the number of talented persons associated with it, there is, in a playful way, a group in the frontier of grasping Toronto, witty and well-informed, not arrogant about their power, but aware of it.

Rather the major domo of the media mafia is Barbara Frum, the frail-but-tough anchor on the most successful news show in Canadian radio history, *As It Happens*, and now filling the same role on television's *The Journal*, which has changed Canada's sex life as surely as the Manhattan blackout did for New Yorkers that famous fecund evening — by sending the entire country, bewildered but later grateful, to bed an hour earlier each night.

Frum throws the best-planned parties in town, the guests chosen as carefully as cashew nuts, in the elegant home, filled with African art, in a Don Mills glade, all wood and glass since it was designed by the former Vancouver architect Ron Thom. The finest compliment that can be paid the house is that it is the only residence in Toronto that looks as if it could be located in Vancouver.

Murray Frum, who grew so bored being a dentist that he went out and became wealthy as a developer, has the sense of humour of (and looks somewhat like) an elongated Woody Allen. Barbara Frum, for all her gentle ways, is a ferocious trader of information, almost equal to the master of all (high praise indeed), Jack Webster. She is very possibly the kindest person in Canada.

Robert Fulford, the erudite editor of *Saturday Night*, appears as a recreation of Edmund Wilson. He is the amused and aloof arbiter of those who write Canadian books, produce films or need intellectual spanking. He is a nonkinky Hugh Hefner, tending his Bunnyland of print.

When Peter Lougheed wanted to infiltrate Toronto and burrow into the soft underbelly of Central Canada dogma on his energy fight with Ottawa, he was able to find an entree into the group to apply the message/massage. Trial lawyer Julian Porter, son of an Ontario chief justice, chairman of the Toronto Transit Commission, a light-reined toucher of the levers of power, long-sought as an ideal Tory candidate for any high position up to premier, was the key to the lock.

Anna Porter, his wife, sees herself as the female reincarnation of Maxwell Perkins, the famous American bookman who nurtured and encouraged F. Scott Fitzgerald, Thomas Wolfe and Hemingway, covering their debts, stroking their inadequate egos, picking up their laundry, buying them eggs. (Was Perkins appreciated? No. Did he brood about it? No.)

Lougheed could be introduced at dinner parties to such card-carrying liberals as Fulford and Adrienne Clarkson, the stunning intellect from CBC television who is now Bill Davis' secret weapon in Paris; as Ontario's agent-general, she has the overshadowed Quebec ambassador at Parisian cocktail parties impaling himself on his own swizzle stick.

He could even meet, across the canapés, such regular members of the group as Peter Herrndorf, English network vice-president of the very CBC that Lougheed was suing because of its rough treatment of him in its *Tar Sands* docudrama. It might even have something to do with the fact that, the day the libel trial was to open in Edmonton early this year, the Holy Mother Corp. and the premier made a settlement on the courtroom steps, Lougheed accepting $82,500 in damages. Dinner party companions come to understand each other.

The analogy is not exactly like Tom Wolfe's famous account of the Black Panthers being entertained by the radical chic groupies at Lenny Bernstein's New York pad. The point is that a Western Tory premier, wanting to get his message across, has access to the opinion-moulders in the communications capital because there is a vacuum there.

Pierre Trudeau, once the intellectuals' darling, has out of boredom and lassitude alienated most of those who would confess to being of his political persuasion. He doesn't have any ministers, acolytes or outriders (now that Coutts has left) who would be taken seriously in any drawing room or trivia contest around the white wine and salmon. Fleming? Cosgrove? Kaplan?

Those far-off Conservatives such as Lougheed, and even such local ones as Worthington and Amiel, are allowed to edge their way in, because Ottawa has disappeared as a presence in Toronto.

Pierre Trudeau has let the country's most powerful city slip away from him by not appealing to its talent.

9
Third Digression

Confessions of a Closet Enthusiast

Doesn't Fotheringham like anything?...
well, Oysters Florentine, for openers...
Eric Kierans and Robert Stanfield...
Frank Sinatra-on-records but
not Sinatra-off-records... Jack Webster-
on-the-air but not Webster-off-the-air
...oranges

Constant Reader, pulling himself up short, irritated, asks: "Doesn't Fotheringham like anything?"

As a matter of fact, it is no problem at all to grant this request. Mr. Fotheringham is a closet enthusiast. He likes an absolutely phantasmagorical number of things.

Mr. Fotheringham, it has been learned, likes Kay Starr. Also Oysters Florentine. He likes Ged Baldwin, Karen Kain and Tuborg. Also Robert Morley. It is hard to imagine him getting enough of Guy Lafleur. He also is very much in favour of Don Shirley.

He is absolutely for Kurt Vonnegut, Iona Campagnolo and Jack Shadbolt. On the other hand, he rather dislikes brussels sprouts and Senator Jack Austin. He likes John Crosbie and Roy MacLaren, Eugene Forsey's letters-to-the-editor. He endures Larry Zolf, a good friend.

The rumour around is that Fotheringham is in favour of Chinese food, Peter De Vries and Barbara Frum's husband. In truth, he likes Japanese food more than Chinese food.

He likes Lawrence Durrell and Dover sole. He has a mad pash for Billy Eckstine. He is in favour of tennis but not golf, the second most stupid sport in the world. The most stupid sport in the world is curling.

Mr. Fotheringham favours politicians who speak the truth. He likes Jean Chrétien, Dave Barrett and Richard Hatfield. His regard lessens when they open their mouths in public.

He likes Dylan Thomas and Woody Allen. Also Gilbert and Sullivan. He has always been in favour of Mary McCarthy. Also sunshine, in moderate amounts. He is in favour of Pommard. Also Cleo Laine, in immoderate amounts.

He obviously likes Max Shulman, also John Charles Thomas, Johann Sebastian Bach, John Robert Colombo. But he is able to restrain his enthusiasm for John Philip Sousa. He is much in favour of Housman, A. E., and likes Siegfreid Sassoon — but likes Wilfred Owen more than Sassoon.

He has always liked John Landy but never much fancied Roger Bannister. He has always been a sucker for the under-dog. He liked Gordie Drillon over Syl Apps, Whirlaway over Alsab, Swaps over Nashua. He likes oranges.

Fotheringham likes Sinatra-on-records, dislikes Sinatra-off-records. He likes Eric Kierans and Robert Stanfield. He is in favour of B. Goodman, A. J. Liebling and Montreal. What he likes most at the moment is John Irving.

He likes Elizabeth Gray's lascivious laugh and Nicole Belanger's malicious wit. He is in love with a lady called Francesca.

He liked the 1968 Trudeau and admires, but does not much like, the 1982 Trudeau. He likes Jack Webster on-the-air, but not Webster-off-the-air. He is in favour of Spike Milligan and salmon. He can take a lot of Joyce Grenfell and a little of Ogden Nash. He likes Rome, born-again New York and Hong Kong.

There is absolutely no limit to the things Fotheringham is enthusiastic about. He likes Carmen McRae, Gore Vidal, E. B. White, Fats Waller, beaches, hockey-in-the-flesh and Billy Graham-on-TV. He does not like hockey-on-TV and thinks Billy Graham-in-the-flesh would be appalling. He likes Joe Clark in a small room, thinks he's a disaster outside it. He likes John Dempsey and Jean-Paul Riopelle.

He is in favour of Flanders and Swann and mourned at

Stanley Holloway. He likes Jacqueline Bissett, even Albert Payson Terhune.

If he could be sure it wouldn't be found out, he might even confess he is in favour of Pierre Berton. He likes John Steinbeck, but not Carol Burnett, Johnny Carson or John McEnroe. In a lifeboat for a length of time, he would prefer as companions Ring Lardner and Peter Ustinov.

He likes green peppers, I. F. Stone, Spain, Anthony Sampson, Sonny Terry and Brownie McGhee, Harry Boyle, Clyde Gilmour, Red Smith's style, Adrienne Clarkson and prawns. He could live on cheese and may have to.

He likes to hear George Burns sing and to read Robert Graves. Constant Reader would be amazed at the number of things about which he is enthusiastic.

I am authorized to speak for Mr. Fotheringham.

10
Manitoba
*The Fun Beneath
the Surface*

Winnipeg, broad-shouldered, rough and garlicky...
talent producer to the eastern world...
wall-to-wall Bunkerism...Beer and Skits...
POPE ELOPES!...Otto Lang,
the Grit's epitaph in the West

Manitoba is the most sedate of the Western provinces, minus the social fervour of Saskatchewan, the buccaneer drive of Alberta, the looniness of British Columbia. This is because of its unfortunate fate in being planted next to Ontario. A portion of the Central Canada pomposity and turgidity has rubbed off, by osmosis seeping across the border. There is fun beneath the Manitoba surface, but there is that half-Ontario glaze over it.

Manitoba has changed premiers, going from the Conservatives' Sterling Rufus Lyon, who was so mean it was rumoured he threatened to tax the rubber tips on crutches, to the NDP's Howard Pawley, whose idea of fun on a Saturday night is to go down to Eaton's and try on gloves.

Rufus Lyon. There is a fine middle name. Manitoba specializes in this. When Duff Roblin resigned as premier in 1967 to joust unsuccessfully with Robert (Banana) Stanfield for Dief's job, he was succeeded by a portly undertaker from Minnedosa, one Walter Weir — known, naturally, as Minnedosa Fats. A young reporter, diligently doing his job, went to his newspaper library to find out the full name of the new premier so it could be used in all its dignified glory.

There was no mention in Weir's campaign literature of a middle name. The diligent reporter dug deeper. No mention.

117

The further he dug, the more apparent it was that Walter Weir, or his handlers, had buried his full name.

By now fascinated with the mystery, the scribe pursued his quest and — finally — found his evidence. Walter Weir's middle name? Cox-Smith. *Beautiful!* A politician going from platform to platform, rally to rally, forever fearful that an opponent might reveal to the world that he is a Cox-Smith! Our hearts went out, immediately, to undertaker Walter Weir and, on second thought, to his mother.

The dying Manitoba Liberals had a leader called Bobby Bend, and it was suggested that the appropriate election slogan would be: "Go Round the Bend with Bobby."

Winnipeg is a broad-shouldered town, rough and garlicky. The economy is going nowhere, but the city has no self-doubts. While Vancouver gazes, fascinated, in its mirror, and Montreal glances sardonically at grasping Toronto, and Toronto is stricken with awe of New York, Winnipeg is serene, oblivious, profane. It does not envy anybody. It is civic karma.

It produces a steady stream of talent that goes to Toronto and beyond and muscles its way through the media. There is Larry Zolf, offspring of the Marx Brothers (Groucho and Karl); writer Jack Ludwig; critic Martin Knelman; publisher James Lorimer; CBC heavy Peter Herrndorf; Stratford Festival saviour John Hirsch; Tom Hendry, a large influence in the Toronto theatre world.

There is Danny Finkleman, the CBC's licensed eccentric; Adele Wiseman, Beryl Fox, Melinda McCracken. There is Scott Young followed by Neil Young, Trent Frayne, Martin O'Malley, sportswriter Jim Coleman, Ian Sinclair of Canadian Pacific — not to forget the immortal Deanna Durbin.

Winnipeg is wall-to-wall Bunkerism, delighting in raunchy insults that cut across its own racial smorgasbord. When Governor-General Ed Schreyer was elected premier in 1969 (Minnedosa Fats had called a snap election right in the midst of an NDP leadership race), he had French-Canadian René Chartier as his executive assistant and cabinet ministers named Cherniack, Uskin, René Toupin, Rev. Philip Petursson, Burtniak and Borowski.

As a litmus paper test of the town, there is the strange phenomenon of the annual Winnipeg Beer and Skits, the last remaining stag social event in Canada. It is a tribal affair that is the forerunner of the much tamer Ottawa Press Gallery annual dinner and show where cabinet ministers are speared and savaged.

Winnipeg is a throwback — there is a touch of 1940s to the place — and one thousand of the upwardly mobile men in town fight to get tickets to this annual production where Kotex jokes are still considered funny. At a time when females now constitute a good half of any newsroom in the country, the Winnipeg Press Club (filled with women) still bans them from its show. Winnipeg is a throwback.

No one is spared at Beer and Skits. I once sat beside Sterling Rufus Lyon when he was the star target in a skit patterned after *One Flew Over the Cuckoo's Nest*. A doctor in the insane asylum explains that before "the little redheaded fart can be given a lobotomy, we'll have to give him a brain transplant." Lyon beamed bravely, as did Manitoba's lieutenant-governor, who sat down the table.

A prominent lawyer, underlining Winnipeg's cultural strength, did a number in which he explained that Scotch is the only liquor named after a people. "After all, can you buy a mickey of Kraut? A bottle of Bohunk? A fifth of Frog? How about a crock of Wop? A jug of Chink? You can't even get a jigger of Nigger?"

They loved it — including a black member of the cast. It brought down the house. Winnipeg doesn't take itself seriously. (Ottawa does, in spades, and Calgary is getting there.)

A star turn most years is the legendary John Robertson, a Winnipeg character who has twice won National Newspaper Awards but is better known as the subject of song and story in the press bars of the land. At forty-eight, he no longer drinks but, as we say, still has a high lifetime average.

He received his early notoriety by writing such headlines as WORMS GET EARLY BIRD — on the death of the local president of the Early Bird Co. He once caused *Winnipeg Tribune* publisher Ross Munro a near heart attack by running off a few bogus front pages that featured in giant type: POPE ELOPES!

His most famous caper came after he had chased *Toronto Telegram* publisher John Bassett around his office desk "while in the grip of the grape." Later, cold sober, to demonstrate how easily it could be done, he playfully composed a sports story that spelled out — in the leading initial of each paragraph — a message that read: Fuck You, Everybody. It made the paper. Goodbye, Toronto Tely.

In Montreal, he so inflamed listeners of his radio show by rallying more than a hundred thousand signatures protesting Robert Bourassa's language law that he had sixteen bomb threats in one day and his children had to be escorted to school by bodyguards.

On the *Winnipeg Tribune* one Christmas, news editor Al Rogers received a police report on a young man named Oliver who had been stabbed in the vital parts by his wife. He threw it to Robertson to write the headline. Robertson returned it with: YOU SHOULD HAVE SEEN OLIVER TWIST.

Rogers told him to get serious so they could make it to the press club before closing time. Walking there through the snow, Rogers casually asked what he finally wrote. Robertson confessed: SHE DECKED THE HALLS WITH BALLS OF OLLIE.

They sprinted back to the paper and had the presses stopped.

The Dr. Hunter S. Thompson of Canadian journalism ballooned to 260 pounds — "The only exercise I got was climbing the press club steps" — before he decided to save himself from his suicidal lifestyle. He covered the Boston Marathon, and the sight of all those healthy bodies snapped something inside him. Two years later he was back in Boston — to run the race with his fourteen-year-old son.

He finished. He runs forty miles a week. He has raised more than $1 million for the Manitoba mentally retarded. He is a born-again jogger.

He became close to Terry Fox and was with him when Fox

had to end his epic run outside Thunder Bay. The one-legged boy told Robertson, "For God's sake, don't wait all your life if you want to do something. Do it before it's too late."

After Fox's death, Robertson as the $74,000-a-year host of Winnipeg's nightly CBC-TV show received a call in late 1981 from Manitoba Senator Nate Nurgitz, suggesting there might be an open Tory nomination in St. Vital, a Winnipeg suburb. Sterling Rufus Lyon hadn't called the election yet, but Robertson recalled Terry Fox and decided to do something.

He was already into taping some pre-election gems: "Sterling Lyon does the work of two men — Laurel and Hardy." Instead, he resigned the $74,000 and the stoic Lyon was there on the platform the night Robertson took the nomination by acclamation — telling his audience he had been out door-knocking "with a bottle of German shepherd-remover in my hand."

He was trounced, of course, as Howard Pawley's NDP swept Sterling Rufus out of power. The CBC could hardly take back a $74,000 defeated political candidate. In his latest reincarnation, John Robertson has joined the *Toronto Sun* as a sportswriter. To greet him, sports editor George Gross wrote "Welcome John Robertson" — spelled out in the leading initial of each paragraph in his column.

Winnipeg is basic. Ed Schreyer, when he ran Manitoba, lived in a house beside the railway tracks, just past the Esso refinery, which the premier bought at a tax sale after the bootlegger owner had skipped town. Farley Mowat parked his camper in the backyard — and stayed all summer.

My favourite story about His Excellency, Governor-General Edward Schreyer, and Her Excellency, Lily Schreyer, involves the time they decided to leave the four children at home and holiday on a leisurely drive through northern Manitoba. They stopped for gas in a small town and who should appear as the gas jockey but Sylvester, who as a boy had been one of Lily Schreyer's dates.

As Sylvester moved to the rear of the car to fill the tank, Ed Schreyer, with a small grin, said, "Just imagine where you'd be today if you had married him."

Lily Schreyer thought a moment, staring straight ahead, and said, "If I had married him, today I would be the wife of the premier of Manitoba."

Winnipeg is also the home now of Adrian Lang, indefatigable wife of Otto Lang, the last strong Liberal minister from the Prairie provinces where the party is now in oblivion. The incredibly slim-waisted Adrian, named after the last English pope, had the final of her seven children by age twenty-eight — "I wanted nine, but ran out of husband." In her heady whirl through Ottawa in the early Trudeau days as a foil to her stoic husband, she was known as "the power behind the drone."

The dominant — and first — skyscraper in Winnipeg was built by the James Richardson grain people and it sits, naturally, at Portage and Main, which used to be the crossroads of Canada (where now pedestrians are fined if they attempt to walk across the famous intersection rather than using the underground walkway). The tower has the choice clients — Price Waterhouse, Sun Life, Coopers & Lybrand, Midland Doherty, Merrill Lynch — with the Richardsons taking up the top six floors of the thirty stories. On the twenty-fifth floor sits the onetime boy wonder of Prairie politics, Otto Lang, now the executive vice-president of Pioneer Grain Co. Ltd.

He's an epitaph for the Liberal party in Western Canada. A whiz at school, a Rhodes Scholar, dean of the University of Saskatchewan's law school while still in his early thirties, Otto Lang had a steady rise through the Trudeau cabinet (not helped greatly by Adrian, early on, confiding to a journalist that "Trudeau says Otto is the smartest man in the cabinet").

His much-publicized use of government jets (My Nanny Flies Over the Ocean) and his fights with feminist forces over abortion didn't hurt him as much as his association with a party that was seen in Saskatchewan as completely aloof and Ottawa-bound. He finished a humiliating third in Saskatoon in 1979 to his own priest, the NDP's Rev. Bob Ogle.

Now out of the cabinet, out of politics, out of his own province, Lang's job is to get the crop of Pioneer, the largest independent grain company outside the Wheat Pool, to its terminals in Vancouver, Thunder Bay and Sorel, Quebec. He has to do this under the realization that Prairie farmers, after all these decades under Liberal rule, do not grow anywhere near what they could for a hungry world since Ottawa has never been able to structure a transportation system that can get the grain to the ships that would send it overseas.

Lang, once a transport minister himself, sees the frustration through new eyes as a Westerner. He'll never be back in politics because he knows, as a Liberal, he is dead in the region of his roots. When a man just turned fifty realizes that, it's a measure of how far the Liberals have fallen.

Lang now works for the Richardsons, and they sent their own contribution, Jimmy, to the Trudeaucrats with monumentally disappointing results. James Richardson, from the silk-stocking riding of Winnipeg South, went to Ottawa in the Trudeaumania sweep of 1968 and moved through his cabinet duties in a resolutely pedestrian fashion.

Richardson always strolled to his own drummer (he stopped going to Beer and Skits after complaining to a companion that he didn't get the jokes) and became increasingly alienated from the thrust of the Trudeau cabinet. He finally left the Liberal ranks in 1976 over differences he has never been able to explain in understandable terms but which centre on the fact that he doesn't really like bilingualism. He wanders the political wilderness, rather like Paul Hellyer in his own serene belief that no one really understands him, showing up at federal-provincial conferences, eager to talk to reporters who pay him no mind, an undiscovered prophet.

Richardson finished himself off as being taken seriously by anyone influential when, as defence minister, he submitted himself to a long conversation with reporter Marci McDonald, who was doing a profile on him for *Maclean's*, while on a trans-Atlantic flight in a government plane. The Atlantic is a large ocean. Richardson relaxed with a few drinks and, among the gaucheries that tumbled forth one startling one stood out.

It was that he was rather tired of the complaints of Indians. After all, they had spent all those centuries, before the white man arrived in North America, dragging their belongings on "two sticks" behind their ponies instead of having the wit to invent the wheel.

James Richardson, millionaire, mystic, politician-without-a-party, has thereafter been known in every press and political gathering in the land as "Jimmy Two-Sticks."

The mantle of Liberal heavyweight in Manitoba has fallen upon the thick locks of Lloyd Axworthy, the white hope of Winnipeg until he forgot to count and neglected to remind himself that more than fifty percent of Canadians are female. The eldest of the four Axworthy boys, he has been greatly influenced by his stint at Princeton (at least his wardrobe has) in the Kennedy days.

He has a voice that comes out of the bottom of a rain barrel and is thought to believe that a sense of humour is something found in the Criminal Code. He is known in press circles as "Tank McNamara" — after the comic strip jock announcer.

A supporter of John Turner in past days, he was actually talked of as potential leadership material in late 1979 before Mr. Trudeau rolled back the stone and resurrected himself. Axworthy never recovered from his stiff-necked confrontation with feminist forces on the Status of Women and the Ottawa joke was that he was going downhill faster than Steve Podborski.

Axworthy's mistake was in taking on Doris Anderson, who is herself from the Prairies and has never taken a backward step in a fight with anyone, having left the Maclean-Hunter empire when she felt she could not rise in a male oligarchy, even after her outstanding success as editor of *Chatelaine*.

Anderson was the government-appointed president of the Canadian Advisory Committee on the Status of Women — termed in some quarters as Broads Canada. When this appellation appeared in a newspaper column, a small rat pack of Ottawa female shovers and makers — Anderson; Elizabeth Gray, now the *As It Happens* husky-throated host; Nicole Belanger, now executive producer of *Morningside*; Pam Wallin, now the *Canada AM* star; Stevie Cameron, the Ottawa gossipist supreme; Sondra Gotlieb, now the resident star of the Canadian

Embassy in Washington — met in a weekly gathering that they described as a Broads Canada lunch at the National Arts Centre restaurant, overlooking the Rideau Canal. With such massive media guns aimed at his innards, Axworthy didn't have a hope.

There are those of suspicious mind in Ottawa who wondered about the rather puzzling Axworthy appointment in the first place, saddling with the responsibility for women's rights a rookie minister who was going through a marriage breakdown himself and whose views on feminism could be fairly well assessed. Was Lloyd Axworthy set up? Or just tested?

His younger brother Tom is the prime minister's principal secretary, succeeding to that post when Jimmy Coutts did his spectacular pratfall in Spadina. Moustachioed, as witty as Lloyd is dour, he rather resembles a bear being rolled down a hill. He has taught at Eton during summer holidays and is a treasure-house of political trivia. A young lady in Ottawa once asked, "How come Lloyd got all the teeth, hair and voice and Tom got the brains?"

The younger Axworthy is a great fan of the Montreal Expos and in his livelier days was almost personally responsible for the annual profit of Mamma Teresa's, a downtown Ottawa restaurant much given to spaghetti stains and late-night cabals. The place became temporarily famous during the constitution arm-wrestling when aides of Ontario's Bill Davis stumbled upon some emissaries of Saskatchewan's Allan Blakeney one night and, over the groceries and some grape, devised a few of the constitutional compromises that supposedly solved all our problems (while leaving out the one-quarter of the country that lives in Quebec). The informal pact immediately became known as the Cannelloni Accord, and it is said that Axworthy has had three red-checked tablecloths, scene of some of his earlier wars, made into family crests in honour of the Pasta Pact.

It is Axworthy who is behind the attempt of the Trudeaucrats to shift the party to the left, particularly on the Prairies, so as to hold off the charging NDP which has succeeded the Liberals as the second party in that portion of the world. The NDP has regained power in Manitoba — Sterling Rufus having blown it all in one term with his Reaganomics — and has an even chance to do the same in British Columbia.

The major thrust and drive in the NDP caucus in Ottawa now come from a gang of young and cocky MPs from the West: Bill Blaikie from Manitoba; Lorne Nystrom from Saskatchewan; and Ian Waddell, Svend Robinson, Nelson Riis and Jim Fulton from B.C. That is Ed Broadbent's major problem — his power base is the dying automobile unions in Oshawa in a province, Ontario, where manufacturing is bleeding profusely, while his caucus is increasingly from Western Canada.

Tom Axworthy, attempting to keep the Grits clinging by their fingertips in the West until perhaps a new leader can remove the hatred, has devised an alliance with the credit unions as a means of undercutting the NDP. The political science theories of the underling are supposed to compensate for the airy attitude of the boss, who views most everything west of Kenora as a wasteland of intellect, a desert of the mind.

The Liberal party has failed in the West because the man who leads it, coming from a different culture and a different region, has never really attempted to understand Western Canada. It puzzles him, and he throws up his famous shrug, a brilliant mind pockmarked with petulance. If he had invested as much effort trying to solve his bewilderment as Western Canada has in attempting to understand Quebec, there would be a different Liberal party today. In keeping it in power, he has vitiated it.

Axworthy, celebrated away from the office for his one-liners, epitomizes something else about Trudeau. Both Axworthy and his predecessor, Coutts, were star catches at Ottawa parties because of their sense of humour — a quality foreign to the man they worked for.

Pierre Trudeau has wit, as the Irish (Wilde and Shaw, Brendan Behan) have. But he has no sense of humour, as the English have. Wit is directed at others. Sense of humour involves oneself. The droll Robert Stanfield, who could never project in public, each year in Ottawa consistently wiped out Trudeau in the jesting contests at the black-tie Parliamentary

126

Press Gallery dinner. He could make fun of himself, the whole point of these incestuous, in-joke cabarets. Trudeau, reading in bored fashion the constructions of his joke-writers, mistiming the punch lines, cannot. The man who vowed as a boy that he would never allow anyone to hurt him, to intrude on his space, will not allow humour that privilege. He seems genuinely puzzled at so many of the broad-stroking skits, the despairing gallery president having to explain the jokes to him.

(Stanfield, after leaving Ottawa, broke his leg when his sailboat, which he was helping to carry down to the lake, fell on him. When acquaintances spotted the cast and asked the inevitable what-happened question, he replied, deadpan: "Hit by a boat." Puzzled frowns. "Yes," was that celebrated painful drawl. "Got to stop walking on the lake.")

While Axworthy is an antic wit, as funny about his own party as he is about his political enemies, Coutts is renowned as a mimic, a Mickey Rooney-sized cherub who delights dinner parties with his well-honed impersonations of Paul Martin; of the partisan elf, Jack Pickersgill; of Trudeau himself.

There is a strange *discontinuity* — not just between Trudeau and his two most recent witty advisers — but with the entire record of those who have guided the prime minister since 1968. A man noted for the severe discipline of his own mental processes, he seems easily steered when it comes to policy. He keeps himself as tightly sealed as a can of clams but is peculiarly supine in the pure political sense.

A historian reading his report card will determine that he has been all over the map, a chap wandering the Sahara of Liberal principles like a punch-drunk wanderer staggering about in search of water. There is no fixed star in his public career — as opposed to his private.

Charles Lynch, the Southam columnist, once called Trudeau "a physical fitness nut with a high I.Q." That's not bad. He's not really a politician, but a dazzling personality who dabbles in good works. He always exudes a certain contempt for the common toil of politics and relies on idea men to shape the mould he then polishes. A Churchill he ain't, a Roosevelt he ain't, even a Mackenzie King he ain't.

His career, once he had achieved power, has been remarkably guided by those who have his ear. He is the persona, the star who glistens like the morning sun, but behind him someone else is always steering. For a brilliant mind, he wobbles all over the spectrum once you look at his overall direction.

The principal secretary to the prime minister is the second most powerful man in Ottawa, and therefore in Canada. Cabinet ministers cower before him, mandarins bow and mere mortals quake. He is the gatekeeper to the presence of Himself. He who controls access controls power. When Alexander Haig confided to Richard Nixon that he no longer had pre-eminence in access to Ronnie Reagan, Nixon told him it was ball game over and advised him to quit. Haig quit. In Ottawa, the principal secretary is a supreme being — Haldeman and Ehrlichman wrapped up in one chubby ball.

When Trudeau became prime minister in 1968, he hired for the post Marc Lalonde, a granitic mind — like Trudeau — who had been a lawyer advising the government on constitutional matters. In private, Lalonde can charm the wax from bees, but in official dealings he is cold and ruthless.

He ran Trudeau's office with an iron hand, made a boatload of enemies and the Grits, with all their flow-charts and beautiful people, slid steadily from 1968 to 1972 near-defeat.

Strangely enough, Lalonde was Trudeau's last Francophone principal secretary, all the successors being Anglophones — supervising the process by which their boss has progressively lost support in the Western half of the country where it now does not own a single provincial seat and only two federal.

In 1972, despite having been frightened to death by the electorate, Trudeau decided to use the vital principal secretary post as an unemployment office. Lalonde having been elected, the title was used as welfare for Martin O'Connell, a dull Toronto cabinet minister who had been defeated and was in need of groceries. Mr. Trudeau, the shining star whose compass had gone astray, was persuaded that the party needed rebuilding, and so a carpenter was sufficient.

By 1974, the nonsparkling Mr. O'Connell safely returned to the House of Commons, there was the need for a new body. It was another eccentric choice, a clever brain from Vancouver, Jack Austin, who had ambitions as long as his controversial career in legal and mining circles. His imagination ranged widely, as evidenced by his key role in formulating Canada's part in the uranium cartel while serving as deputy minister in the department of energy, mines and resources.

One could never discern any pattern in Trudeau's basic political philosophy in flipping from the fierce drive of Lalonde to a defeated politician to the skittering mind of Austin. What was the direction? Where was the link? As many of us had predicted, the gathering questions about Austin's background forced him to the ejector seat into the Senate after just fifteen months in the job. Trudeau's lack of care in the selection process remained as puzzling as ever.

Next choice was Coutts, out of the slick Toronto consulting field, forced on the compliant Trudeau by the party pros, who wanted more manipulation. One is reminded of the woman, married three times, who was asked by a female friend to describe her husbands. The first one, she explained, was a homosexual and it obviously didn't work. The second was a deviant and that was simply ridiculous. The third one, she said, was a public relations man and all he did was sit on the edge of the bed every night telling her how good it was going to be.

However, we digress. Coutts delivered the manipulation, steering the product Trudeau this way and that, ordering him to shut up during election campaigns, blocking interviews with the dreaded press. It was Coutts who arranged the buying of Jack Horner, the super-cynical move that sealed the death of the Liberals in the West.

With Coutts gone down the sump hole of Spadina, Trudeau simply picked his assistant, Tom Axworthy. He is on the reformist left wing of a party that, after selling out the country to the Americans while under Trudeau, is now trying to buy it back under the same PM. It is interesting that the prime minister's last three principal secretaries have been from Western Canada — and that half of the country has increasingly become contemptuous of him. If they can't teach him, who can?

There's a strange indifference to Trudeau in picking his major aides. He seems not only a bad judge of talent, but an indifferent judge. He has stern views on the constitution and language — but surprisingly docile ones on the economy, i.e., how most people live.

He dazzles, but he has no direction outside his constitution obsession. It's a severe mind, but steered — like a raft on a muddy pond — by a changing crew of boys.

11
Saskatchewan
The Unconscious Force

The meaning of distance out here . . .
a fey wish that Trudeau, Lalonde and Pépin
would travel this road . . . Dr. Foth
is soft on Saskatchewan; he was born there . . .
Tommy Douglas at CCF picnic . . .
Some new Vulgarians . . .
the Uke and Toque Show

The purest water in the world is the water that collects in shallow dips in wheat fields in the late spring. The ponds are the reflected blue of the unending prairie sky and are always scalloped with little ripples from a breeze, origin unknown.

It is a standard thing, of course, to bemoan the ugliness of the Prairies but in fact at this time of year the land is quite pretty. There have been these late rains and the wheat is lush and green, perhaps ten inches high. There is that strange feeling, for someone from the mountains, of looking around and seeing the horizon in a 360-degree sweep. It is as if a Plexiglas dome has been set down on a flat surface.

Just as surely as in the Moroccan desert, or in the medieval remains of southern Italy, you can detect the settlements of humans from the small pockets of trees across the landscape. There is the hum — long forgotten — of telephone wires in the silence. You can hear, uninterrupted, the bobolink's truncated trill. White birds as large as seagulls trail tractors across the summer fallow.

The road in front of the car melts into a liquid with the heat haze. One does not need a map since a route ahead can be devised in geometric patterns, the whisper lines of far-off telephone poles providing the guide to where the roads intersect. Off in the distance, the next town can be detected from the wavering forms of the two or three or four grain elevators that dance and sway through the heat.

Saskatchewan people have the best sense of humour in the land. It is the Regina airport terminal and two teen-age blond boys in shorts, brimming with rural health, stand watching the incoming passengers. Suddenly they sprint forward to a man coming through the entrance, shouting "Daddy! Daddy!" The entire crowd in the small terminal turns to watch the tender emotion. The poor embarrassed man they hold their arms out to is black. An old friend. That's Saskatchewan humour — broad, for public consumption.

There's a bit of prejudice riding on this, you must understand. Dr. Foth was born there, in a little town called Hearne (you remember it, on the Soo Line, some fifty miles south of Moose Jaw, near Rouleau, Briercrest and Avonlea — home of the curling world-champion Campbell brothers).

People from Hearne are called Hearnias. The town was so small we couldn't even afford a village idiot. Everyone had to take turns. (Eventually, however, I moved to British Columbia, which improved the I.Q. of both provinces.)

I went to a one-room schoolhouse, twelve grades in one room, on the bald prairie. We small ones would stand, in anticipation every morning, at the gate as the big hitters of the school raced in on their ponies, the hero-worship reserved for the boy with the most wild-looking pinto stallion, just as the adulation goes now for the smoothie who tools up to a high school with the biggest mufflers mounted on muscle wheels.

The only other person in my grade was Kenny Newans. When we finished our sums we were allowed to go outside and snare gophers, while teacher went on to the higher grades. I seem to have spent most of my early grades outside, snaring gophers. One of us would pour a bucket of water down one end of a gopher hole. When the creature popped up at the other end, soaking and indignant, he would be snared around the neck with a length of binder twine. This proved educational for later use in political journalism.

Kenny Newans is now sports director of Calgary televi-

134

sion station CFCN. Which means that of two boys raised in a one-room schoolhouse in the midst of the Depression, one earns his living from his pen and the other with his mouth. Must be something in that old time religion after all. Either that, or it must be useful spending a lot of time around gophers.

The trees on the road west from Winnipeg are gold, stolen from the brush of Cézanne. The prairie at this time of year, suspended in Indian summer, is not dull and bland at all but delicate and beautiful. A traveller on the road west, swallowing the miles between the glimpses of civilization, contemplates only one fey wish. It is that the stern intellects in the Liberal cabinet — Trudeau, Lalonde, Pépin — could travel this road just once to comprehend what distance means to the West.

In these fathomless miles, skies stretching to the horizon in all directions, is the basic Western Canadian belief in land and property and resources. Distance from one's neighbours creates a feel for the earth. Geography becomes a friend, not an enemy. Form dictates content.

The road dips and waves past Portage la Prairie. Towns called Sidney and Melbourne — how did *they* get here? — disappear behind. Carberry, Justice, Two Creeks. We miss Pope, Snowflake and Rapid City. The problem, with the Ottawa mind-set, is the absence of empathy toward the Western feeling on resource ownership. It is one thing not to agree. It is another thing not to understand. The road extends, wavering but never varying from its westward destination, on through the hours.

It is not a concept easily grasped by sophisticated men from tightly packed urban centres in Montreal or Toronto. The miles pound by, the dead porcupine by the road, the squished skunk, the small animals melded into the asphalt. In Central Canada, one gets on airplanes to travel short distances. Out here, one must travel the land. It sets up a bond. The argument over resources is between men who sit in offices and men who have a feeling for the earth.

In the beverage room in the hotel in Moosomin, Sask., there is no talk of constitution as the snooker balls click. The

135

lady in the green sweater borrows ten dollars from her man as she sets out on the most important project in Canada this day: it is the afternoon she conducts thirty-nine Brownies on a hike.

Outside Wapella, past Red Jacket, an object lesson thunders by. A freight train headed back east, its lengths and lengths of automobile carriers empty as it heads to Windsor and Oakville for its next load. One can see Peter Lougheed smiling. His point, exactly. Hewers of wood and drawers of water.

The clouds scud close to the horizon, deformed white blimps against the blue. The Liberals, now an urban party that flies in planes rather than rides in cars, are genuinely puzzled by all the antagonism. They should travel this road.

At Oakshela, the sky darkens, the wind that warns of approaching winter whips the loose soil from the fields, creating a Sahara dust cloud. The wind dies, the windshield reappears. The big trucks dominate the road, creating their own slipstreams and a shuddering blast of air as they thunder by, their jockeys perched on high, steering their rigs like captains at sea, a sea of stubble and hay that stretches as far as the eye can see. The tourists are gone, the swaying trailers fled safely south.

Near Grenfell, a half-dozen giant loaves of bread loom on the horizon, supermarket icons marching off the TV screen. They prove to be, as distance shrinks, storage loaves of fodder, ten yards high, in symmetry. Another train heads eastward, tank cars from Alberta Gas Chemicals, destined for processing in Central Canada rather than the West. One sees Peter Lougheed's smile expanding to a smirk as the imaginary Trudeau/Lalonde/Pépin stand by this road and see resources flowing ever eastward to those who will profit by them. It's an educational road.

Summerberry goes by. Sintaluta. Kipling, Peebles and Odessa are to the left. Gerald, Esterhazy and Stockholm to the right. The farmers, light-years away from the dust bowl, sit on their space age harvesting machines, technicolor in hue, five-figure in value, air-conditioned, tape deck blaring in the earphones. There is no longer awe for men in vests in Ottawa offices that have double doors for security's sake.

136

The road reaches west. Outside Indian Head, a small airfield holds private planes for these newfound entrepreneurs and landholders who zoom away to potash fields and, one suspects, Arizona. There is no inferiority complex left from the blow-dirt days. Only a sort of weary contempt — and sadness — for those from less changing circumstances who have no idea how once-colonial regions have changed.

Pilot Butte approaches. In Regina, the New York touring company of the Fats Waller Broadway production approaches. Somewhere out there await Conquest, Congress and Climax, Cut Knife, Renown, Outlook, Mozart, Plenty, Unity and Holdfast, Elbow and Eyebrow, Divide, Liberty and Love. The clouds clipper along, lowering to the horizon that never ends and stretches forever.

One only wishes that there were three hitchhikers on this road, learning the lessons of geography, away from the pavement and the airline terminals and the chauffeured limousines. The tumbleweed languidly collides with the front of the car and disintegrates.

> "I feel that here I have made at least a brief acquaintance with the kind of unconscious force which Tolstoy believed is decisive in history."
>
> Hugh MacLennan
> on his 1961 visit to Saskatchewan

Three frisking pinto ponies surge and bump on the grassy slope until they are frozen on the crest against the endless blue sky, like a tableau out of an Old West canvas. In the picnic grounds below, a half-dozen miles northeast of Regina, there are those endless straw boaters, in pastel, adorning the cautious men who wear both belt and suspenders. The plastic folding chairs seek the shade beneath the trees as the old-time fiddle contest begins to tap toes in the rising dust. The horseshoes clank. It is, for one final time, "an old-fashioned CCF picnic," designed to honour the last of the happy warriors, Tommy Douglas, who will not pass this way again, it being 1978 and he does not plan to run again.

137

Tommy Douglas at this point is seventy-three (like all men of passionate belief, he appears perhaps fifty-three in energy) and there has been a tendency to denigrate him, to regard with wry amusement his outdated marionette mannerisms and dismiss his pulpit style.

One suspects, however, that a reassessment is about in order, that the painful progress of social justice in this tremulous country may spotlight just how much this pugnacious bantam accomplished over time that will someday be perceived as pioneering law, but today is taken for granted.

He is the same five-foot-six as when he was lightweight boxing champ of Manitoba. That carefully tended pompadour bounces above the chipmunk grin. His style was a little too evangelical, too corny ever to make him truly comfortable in skeptical British Columbia where he retreated in 1962 after his galling defeat in Regina, first to a Vancouver suburb, then, defeated again, to his Vancouver Island riding.

But this is his turf here, this picnic, these roots. His barbecued chicken dinner grows cold in the waiting Winnebago while he tries to work his way through the faithful who've driven from all over Saskatchewan for this final chance to grasp the wee chap who gave this province back its pride. "If I'd slept on all the kitchen floors of all the farmhouses as claimed here today," he sighs as he chews on his chicken, "I'd have been around more than Casanova."

Saskatchewan is probably the most misunderstood province of all. Ralph Allen, the man from Oxbow, once wrote of "the union of a very old land and a very young people. . . . The Prairies are older than the Nile, older than the hills of Jerusalem, older than Galilee and the Valley of the Jordan." A million years ago, mile-high glaciers began the process that has produced this silt-rich bread basket.

When Tommy Douglas in 1944 became head of the first socialist government in North America, Saskatchewan had the highest per capita debt in Canada, the second-lowest per capita income. There were a total of 138 miles of paved highway in the entire province. Of one hundred thousand farms, some three hundred were electrified.

Over the distance of time, Douglas' seventeen years as premier were indeed a test pattern for what has happened everywhere else: first Bill of Rights in Canada; first supplementary old age pension; first loan plan for small business; first student aid program; first assistance to the arts — a decade before the Canada Council.

Today, Regina and outskirts have that familiar, pleasantly sated look of upward mobility so prevalent in Alberta, British Columbia and Ontario. M. J. Coldwell, when he met the young Baptist preacher Douglas in Weyburn during the birth of the CCF, was outraged at finding Depression families who had nothing to eat but stewed gophers and coffee made from barley. Now, one of the party's aides from Weyburn worked on the Jimmy Carter campaign, learning about computerized telephone lists. The Regina Inn features a minor Hollywood name in a dinner-theatre production of *Same Time, Next Year*, the Bernie Slade Broadway classic on how-to-do-it adultery for the middle class.

What Saskatchewan (and Douglas and the CCF) are most celebrated for, of course, is the introduction of medicare. While nervous Ottawa waffled, the audacity of Douglas was rather breathtaking. He did it, in fact, with free enterprise Yanks.

After hiring Dr. Henry Sigerist of Baltimore's Johns Hopkins University, the world's top authority on social medicine, to do a report, Douglas asked him who the best man would be to run such a program in Saskatchewan. "The best possible man" happened to be Dr. Fred Mott, who was untouchable as assistant surgeon-general of the U.S. Army. Douglas phoned *the* U.S. surgeon-general and somehow, with his blarney (the Scottish version) and passion, got a release for Mott who established a scheme that was followed years later by everyone else in tight-assed Canada.

It is somewhat hilarious that the United States, the only advanced country in the world that has yet to introduce medicare (Germany had it in 1896) supplied the two men who enabled socialist Tommy Douglas to lead the way for the rest of nonsocialist Canada.

There are some four thousand victims of nostalgia on the

mellow Sunday afternoon. His earthy barnyard jokes, dropped with the precision of a pianist, are the more appreciated for being so familiar. If J. S. Woodsworth was the saint in politics and Coldwell the gentleman, Tommy was always slightly suspect, when he took over, as the laugher. David Lewis was impatient to take over, as he eventually did, because Douglas did not have that urban radical hate.

Baptists don't hate. (They don't let down any barriers, either.) He has few close friends in or out of politics. He has Irma and he has these adoring Depression groupies. Perhaps the critics should merely regard his record instead. The famed mimic somehow could never handle French, but he was the bravest man in the country in his stubborn stand against the War Measures Act.

The Saskatchewan he left now has potash, uranium and oil, in total income surpassing agriculture and may indeed have more future economic security than any of the four Western provinces. (Saskatchewan's economy grew more than twice as fast as Canada's economy in 1981. Real domestic product rose by 5.1 percent while the Canadian economy grew by 2.5 percent. Net farm income rose by 160 percent; wages, salaries and supplementary labour income went up 13.8 percent. According to the Conference Board of Canada, Saskatchewan is the only one of the ten provinces not running a budgetary deficit. Saskatchewan has a $4.1 million surplus.)

MacLennan wrote: "These days when I visit Saskatchewan I remember how students from the farms starved during the Depression years in order to get an education. I think how these people cooperated, and thereby upheld the dignity of their species." In that, he saw Tolstoy.

Tommy Douglas stands on a picnic table, the pompadour brushing the red and white stripes of the tent. The sky is now black, and jagged lines of lightning pierce the horizon. He has them howling, remembering their misery. He fits this misunderstood province, the province he remade.

Proof of how far Saskatchewan has come is that it too, though not to the level of its two Western neighborrs, has produced some New Vulgarians. There is forty-four-year-old

140

millionaire rancher Colin Thatcher, the energy and mines minister in Premier Grant Devine's new Conservative government. He is the only son of Ross Thatcher, Saskatchewan's last Liberal premier — one more indication that even the progeny are fleeing the party.

Thatcher, called "the J. R. Ewing of Saskatchewan" in the *Globe and Mail*, tools around Regina in his yellow Corvette, tours his fields in an air-conditioned, telephone-equipped farm vehicle or flies off for his winters in Palm Springs.

The headlines have been messy. A bitter divorce from his wife Joanne followed by a lengthy custody battle over son Regan, who then mysteriously disappeared. After continuing court battles — the presiding judge and the warring lawyers all holding press conferences — the child just as mysteriously materialized; the ex-wife was shot in the shoulder by an unknown assailant. All bona fide evidence that the dust bowl has grown up into your basic suburban domestic chaos.

The thoroughly cynical Thatcher has a sign pasted on his office door: "Are you into a change in scene? Would you like new vistas, new horizons? Are you tired of your workmates? Just screw up one more time."

There is Richard Collver, energetic and charming, who single-handedly revived the Tories from their low state but then, with a rush of something to his head, declared himself the head of a new Unionest Party that would separate Western Canada from the rest of the country and join the United States. This loony idea died faster than last year's corn and may have had something to do with the fact that Collver spends much of his time on his properties in Arizona.

Entangled in myriad financial and legal problems, he was fined five hundred dollars after firing a .357 Magnum into the air, while in an exuberant mood, from his apartment window in downtown Regina. (The mysterious Swiss bank account that was unearthed turned out to be, as claimed, for his daughter's education.)

These small indications of egos trying for bit parts in an episode from *Dallas* are proof that Saskatchewan has come of age.

141

An example of the bankruptcy of Liberal spirit and the corruption of Liberal thought is contained in the object lesson of Roy Romanow. Until Grant Devine's Conservatives upset the astounded Allan Blakeney and his NDP in early 1982, Romanow had been Saskatchewan's attorney-general for almost a decade.

He looks as if he dresses out of *Gentleman's Quarterly*, those ice-chip eyes have the lady reporters doing nip-ups, and he has the clean good looks of a Ukrainian Robert Redford. He is as good on the tennis court as he is before a microphone.

Romanow's father came to Canada as an immigrant in the late 1920s, desperately trying to learn rudimentary English on the boat crossing the Atlantic and, as his boatmates were instructed in like manner, practised on one phrase for the immigration officers: "Me Liberal. Me Mike Romanow."

He went to work for the Canadian National Railways as a labourer in Saskatoon, made well aware that the Natural Governing Party had provided him with a job. He became a strong union man and believed in the CCF after its formation. But when elections came, he was "advised" that he had best vote Liberal, since the Liberals were the ones who had let him into the country. There was a hint there, just a nudge of a threat. The senior Romanow voted Liberal. Had to.

Roy Romanow says, "I've never forgotten that."

When it came time to sell Mr. Trudeau's constitutional package, there was Romanow as cochairman with Jean Chrétien of the road troupe that roamed the country in search of agreement from the squabbling premiers and the autocratic feds. They were billed as "The Uke and Toque Show," two rollicking young risers with a gift for after-hours humour.

There was the attorney-general of little Saskatchewan, given equal billing for months with the justice minister of Canada, coming off very well, thank you. Tune in *As It Happens* and there was Saskatoon's Roy, explaining it all to Barbara Frum. Follow every cameraman's boom mike at the elbowing scrum outside the constitutional doors and there was Roy. A Canadian Club podium in Vancouver? There was Roy, reasonable, conciliatory, charming.

142

What did it get him? It got him offers, nudge-nudge and wink-wink from the feds.

Romanow had a problem. The handsome A-G was the most eligible premier-in-waiting in the country. He'd been elected four times in a row. He'd been in the NDP caucus for thirteen years. He was so sensitive about his youth, knocked for being "too young" at twenty-eight when he lost to Blakeney in the leadership contest of 1970 that to this day he refuses to list his birthdate in the Parliamentary Guide.

Ottawa knew the man who would make a fine premier of a half-dozen other provinces was locked in behind Blakeney, some thirteen years older and in no mood to step aside. The feds figured on the galling fact that Romanow, the Number Two, was a native son, proud product of Saskatoon, while Blakeney was a brainy Maritimer who moved on to Saskatchewan via the civil service route after his Rhodes Scholarship days at Oxford.

The Grits wanted to buy Romanow, just as they had bought Conservative Jack Horner, with offers of enticing Ottawa positions. Just as they had appointed Ed Schreyer as governor-general — the first Gee-Gee of ethnic persuasion, from Western Canada, the first appointment from a socialist background — thinking it would help them electorally in Western Canada. It didn't. Voters don't like insulting bribes. Schreyer was a fine appointment, in that it demythologized the ceremonial post, but it didn't have the result at the polls the Grits intended.

Romanow hung in, even when the escaped memo from Privy Council's Michael Kirby revealed that the feds had cynically planned on the federal-provincial constitutional conference failing. The Toque, mortified at the exposed Machiavellian dealings of the Trudeaucrats, thereafter never had quite the same relationship with The Uke.

Mr. Trudeau, with his famed gift for names, in early meetings continually addressed Romanow as "Romanoff" — perhaps mistaking him for "Prince" Mike Romanoff, the Hollywood café society figure.

The Trudeau mind, trapped in an airlock, deals only in

concepts, not in people. He is famous for his carelessness with names; they simply don't matter to him. His present principal secretary, Tom Axworthy, worked in his office for several years as a policy aide and speech-writer before Trudeau could ever remember his name. "Get me the fat guy," was his signal for Axworthy.

When the PM's popularity was waning in the early 1970s and his reputation had taken on an aura of formal sterility, a speech-writing aide suggested a folksy approach as he was about to address steelworkers in Hamilton. It was the time when Hank Aaron was in the headlines as he verged on breaking Babe Ruth's supposedly inviolate record of 714 home runs, and the aide suggested that the PM, who had barely survived his second election, compare himself to Hank Aaron who never quit after two strikes against him.

"Who's Hank Aaron?"

The aide, swallowing, explained that he was the Atlanta Braves slugger about to break Babe Ruth's record.

"Who's Babe Ruth?"

The aide, perspiration emerging, explained who Babe Ruth was. Once apprised of the approach, Trudeau willingly agreed that it was a good ploy for a speech.

Once before the steelworkers, he made his pitch. Yes, his government perhaps hadn't lived quite up to his expectations of 1968 and yes, it may have been a bit disappointing after 1972, but the 1974 election was a third try and, you know, even though Hank Aaron has one strike on him you don't give up on him — even two strikes, because he still has that third swing to come.

"And you know who Hank Aaron is — he's threatening to break the home run record of Baby Ruth."

George Radwanski, now the editor-in-chief of the *Toronto Star*, author of a sympathetic biography of Trudeau, was given more hours of interviews with the private man for the book than any other author or journalist.

The next time he asked a question at a prime ministerial press conference, Trudeau said, "Yes, Jack?" — and looked around in genuine puzzlement at the hilarity in the press theatre.

Trudeau once had a meeting with Dennis McDermott, president of the Canadian Labour Congress, whom he continually referred to throughout the session as "David."

McDermott, a man of no small ego himself as witness the gold chains and coiffed hairstyle, burned inwardly and finally made the elaborate point that "if *I*, Dennis McDermott, were presented with such-and-such a proposal, I can tell you, Mr. Prime Minister, what *I*, Dennis McDermott, would do."

Trudeau listened thoughtfully throughout and, when McDermott had finished, said, "That's a good point, David."

I digress. In the final early-morning cabal that pasted Canada's constitution together (while Quebec's delegation, unwarned, slept across the river in Hull), it was Romanow, Chrétien and Ontario's Roy McMurtry who did the stickum job. This is understandable, since all three are lawyers and all three suffer from the Anthony Eden/John Turner syndrome: growing old while sitting in the waiting room.

McMurtry, a large, slope-shouldered ex-football player with bedroom eyes (they are put to good use; he has six children) has been attorney-general ever since he joined the Bill Davis government. But Davis, who has been at Queen's Park for twenty-three years and premier for eleven, says that he wants to stay around to beat the twenty-seven-year mark of NDP veteran Donald MacDonald, who resigned this summer to allow new NDP leader Bob Rae to contest his seat.

McMurtry is stalled, Chrétien is stalled and the Grits, knowing Romanow was stalled, tried to buy him. They can't grow their own in this territory, so they try to buy others.

Romanow resisted the Ottawa blandishments and, as his reward, was beaten by nineteen votes in the Tory landslide by twenty-two-year-old Jo-Ann Zazalenchuk, a university student who was a gas pump jockey in her father's Petrocan station.

Romanow, as damaged goods, is of no use to the Liberals now. What is useful to remember is that the same party that bullied the father, years later tried to buy the son. These are not nice people. They will be dead for a long time in this territory.

12
Fourth
Digression
Notwithstanding Lawyers

Our pockmarked constitution . . .
the legal imbalance in the land . . .
five of ten premiers are unsullied by an LL.D . . .
a public in awe of mouthpieces

The first thing we do, let's kill all the lawyers.

— *Henry VI, Part II*

The famed lexicographer Patrick Nagle maintains that lawyers can pick fly droppings out of pepper while wearing boxing gloves. As evidence, we have only to look at our pockmarked constitution, still quivering, all full of pinpricks, loopholes, crochet work and glue. Only a nation whose leaders are lawyers could construct a new Magna Charta built on a "notwithstanding" clause.

That is the metaphor for Canada: notwithstanding. A perfect Mackenzie King word. Notwithstanding that it excludes one of our two founding races and the native people, notwithstanding we have a pluperfect lawyer mind.

It is why the most overlooked event of 1982 is that some tiny progress in the creep of civilization has been achieved. We actually acquired a new premier without adding to the legal imbalance of the land. Grant Devine took over Saskatchewan and, glory be, he is not a lawyer. No one seemed to notice it, but those of us put here to supervise the legal profession marked it down as a significant act, just short of Harold Ballard's brain transplant. It means the never-ending struggle to keep our affairs from being dominated completely by nitpickers in laced shoes is still in a holding pattern, not yet swamped beyond repair.

Since Premier Devine is an agricultural economist, it

149

means that a remarkable five of the ten premiers still hold their heads high, unsullied by the millstone of an LL.D. They are allowed to walk about in public, small boys do not stone them and dogs greet them with a friendly wag of the tail. They are a rare breed, these five, due for extinction eventually like the three-toed wombat, and we should cherish them. One cannot remember when the public last received such a break, since the leadership of the land has been dominated for so long by the legal beagles, everyone had lost count.

James Matthew Lee took over Prince Edward Island and, to everyone's surprise, turned out not to be a lawyer. He is a realtor, which is a fancy name for someone who sells houses. William Richards Bennett of British Columbia is not a lawyer on account you gotta attend university to be one, and MiniWac grew so impatient that he didn't finish the niceties of high school, eager to get out and make a million, which he did.

Bennett is a believer in corporate baron Bud McDougald who, when he died, owned most of Canada. McDougald once confessed: "Left school at 14 and I've regretted it all my life. Should have left when I was 12!" The reason Bennett, who was chairman of the Gang of Eight, was fast asleep at 3:00 AM when the "notwithstanding" nonsense was shoe-horned into the final constitutional bargain in a Château Laurier bedroom was that, not being a lawyer, his mind grew exhausted at all the legal mumbo-jumbo and his body gave him a signal. If you listen to lawyers talking for too long, it makes you sterile. You can look it up.

René Lévesque is not a lawyer, but it was a close call. With that Gallic gift of the gab, the courts might have been on overtime. When he was kicked out of Laval law school for smoking, he joined the U.S. Army as a war correspondent, and journalism — not law — must take the blame for what has followed.

Lucky Brian Peckford is not a lawyer. The Newfoundland premier is probably the only passionate high school English teacher in captivity and achieved the satisfaction of shoving across the table the final compromise solution that supposedly solved the constitution muddle. Peckford's brimstone soul is fired like a furnace at the sight of Pierre Trudeau across the federal-provincial table because the Cartesian mind of the PM is so bloodless (Where's Poland?) that it inflames someone who thinks words should be used to communicate, not obfuscate. If Shakespeare hadn't said it, Peckford would have.

A chap called Plato talked of lawyers' "small and righteous" souls. We are run by them. Always have been. Of 242 federal cabinet ministers between 1867 and 1940, forty-eight percent were lawyers. Dr. John Porter, in his monumental *The Vertical Mosaic*, showed how the percentage is increasing and how lawyers are far more prevalent in our political system than in Britain or Australia. There is one office building in downtown Toronto that contains more *QC*s than there are in the British Isles. Lawyers make up fifty percent of all United States senators and representatives and seventy percent of all presidents, vice-presidents and cabinets. Is it any wonder the world is in such a notwithstanding mess?

Keats wrote, "I think we may class the lawyer in the natural history of monsters." We somehow are cowed by monsters, mainly monsters of the language. Ontario's Bill Davis uses words like jungle camouflage, hiding himself as if a Vietnam combat veteran with his voice box as the uniform. When he intones "finally" in one of his short speeches, you can go out for a hamburger and be assured of returning for the final cliché. Saskatchewan's Allan Blakeney always approached the English language carefully, as a bomb-disposal expert creeping up on an explosive car, ever circling, until the bomb defused for lack of air.

Joe Clark expired, among other reasons, because the public was slightly nervous over a chap who — given the choice of two law schools, Dalhousie and the University of B.C. — flubbed them both. Joe's distaste for the law was his greatest gift, but the public is in awe of the mouthpiece. The chances are the next leaders (Macdonald and Turner on one side, Mulroney and Crosbie on the other) will rise from the legal beagles. Notwithstanding. We are brutes for punishment.

13
Alberta

Man-Boys
in the Promised Land

What makes Lougheed ride? . . .
oil, cowboys and nouveau riche swagger . . .
the key to understanding Alberta
is androgen, the male sex hormone . . .
a whiff of Dallas . . .
the specific gravity of Joe Clark's head . . .
Gordon Kesler, the Louis Riel
of the bronco set

In 1938, a ten-year-old boy broke into a twenty-six-room house in Calgary. The mansion, known as Beaulieu, was up for public auction the next day after being seized for tax arrears. The boy was Peter Lougheed, and the reason he broke into the house was that it had been owned by his grandfather, the grandest man in Alberta, and it was the symbol of the family fortune and reputation that had been destroyed.

The house — filled with teak and brass and eight Italian marble fireplaces — had once entertained British royalty and now was being stripped. Peter Lougheed, from a secret hiding place in the house he knew so well, watched as the entire library — volumes bound in leather — went for twenty-two dollars. Peter Lougheed has a long memory, and a low forgiveness factor, to this day.

Any one of us, one suspects, would have been pierced by the experience of that ten-year-old. Those from Quebec have centuries of grievances. Those from Alberta have similar feelings that run back only a few generations, but the bitterness can be equated.

Lougheed's grandfather graduated from Osgoode Hall and articled with a Toronto law firm. When he saw the potential of making a fortune in the West with the building of

Sir John A. Macdonald's transcontinental railway, he persuaded Sir William Van Horne to make him CPR solicitor in Calgary.

His knowledge of CPR plans allowed Jimmy Lougheed to make judicious land purchases. His buildings eventually dominated the Calgary skyline. For several years after 1914, Lougheed was assessed *half* the taxes in the city of Calgary. When he was made Senator Lougheed, he was the youngest member of the Canadian Senate: thirty-five.

There was something uncanny in his maiden speech when he intimated that Calgary could in time replace Ottawa as the capital and went on to state that the province's resources "when developed, I am satisfied, will eventually make Alberta the dominant portion of the Dominion." That was, gentle reader, in 1889 — the last appointment to the Senate Sir John A. would make.

Grandfather's law partner was R. B. Bennett, the prime minister. Grandfather became, in 1916, Sir James Alexander Lougheed, the first and only Albertan ever knighted. When he died, he left a fortune to Lady Lougheed and heirs.

The Depression, as it seared Western Canada more than Ottawa thinkers yet realize fifty years later, ruined the family. The Metropolitan Life Insurance Co. of Ottawa, which held most of the mortgages on the Lougheed properties, made Royal Trust of Montreal the trustee and put Peter Lougheed's father, Edgar, on a "salary."

Edgar Lougheed, complaining bitterly about how his family was "brought to its heels by the callous moneylenders from the East," turned into a drinker. Peter Lougheed's mother, Edna, suffered a nervous breakdown and underwent psychiatric treatment. The magnificent Beaulieu was turned into a residence for the WACs during the Second World War and is now Red Cross headquarters in Calgary.

Peter Lougheed, as a result of his family's humiliation, became a fighter, a constant competitor. As a teen-ager, his nickname was "The Demander," because of his insistence on turning everything into a contest. Harold Millican, a schoolmate who later worked with Lougheed in government, recalls:

"All of his games, whether cowboys and Indians, table tennis or football, were set up as win-or-lose situations."

University of Alberta political scientist Larry Pratt, in *The Tar Sands*, writes: "What Peter Lougheed articulates so well are the politics of resentment, the frustrated aspirations of a second-tier elite for so long dismissed as boorish cowboys, as yahoos with dung on their boots, by the smug, ruling Anglo-French establishment of Ontario and Quebec."

The first time Marc Lalonde travelled by train from Montreal to his national capital in Ottawa, he found that the conductors on the government's railway couldn't speak to him in his own language. He has devoted his years in Ottawa to setting such outrages aright. It's too bad he didn't have the tolerance, when he was energy minister of Canada, to understand other bitter minorities.

Someone who does understand the situation is Richard Milo, sports editor of *Le Devoir*. After the superbly prepared Edmonton Eskimos had humiliated the Hamilton Tiger-Cats in the 1980 Grey Cup game, he wrote of the winners: "They are to Alberta what Les Canadiens used to be to Quebec. They are the flagship, the showcase. They have to win. It means so much to the whole province. Players realize this. Alberta's honor is at stake, as well as the result of a football game."

So true. If a Quebec sportswriter can recognize it, why can't Marc Lalonde and Pierre Trudeau? Because they are prisoners of their own pilgrimage. That same year, in the College Bowl, a contest in Toronto's Varsity Stadium that would decide the Canadian university football championship, the University of Alberta took great pleasure in running up a 35-0 half-time lead over a befuddled University of Ottawa.

At the intermission, the Alberta star, a five-foot-six-inch quarterback by name of Forrest Kennerd, was asked if his team would ease up in the second half and not make the debacle even more embarrassing.

No chance, he replied quite calmly. His team was still smarting over some supposed slight in the Toronto press and, he emphasized, there wasn't the proper respect for the calibre of Western Canadian collegiate football. Furthermore, his mates represented not just Alberta but the whole West. No respect. The Depression complex runs deep. Instead of the usual Dick-and-Jane inanity of these jockdom interviews, we had a little touch of political science.

The pride runs deep. In 1981 the Golden Bears were defending their title (their fourth trip to the championship game in eleven years) against Nova Scotia's Acadia University — which is the exact opposite of the regional authenticity of the Alberta team. Acadia is a football factory. Only twenty-one of its forty-four players were from the Atlantic provinces. Fourteen of them were imported from Ontario, two from Quebec and seven from the United States.

Forty of the fifty-one Golden Bears were born and raised in Edmonton. Only four were from outside the province. They are the expression of a province, not hired mercenaries. (The mercenaries won in the last minute of play.)

The key to understanding Alberta is androgen. Androgen rules business. Androgen permeates politics. Androgen affects Alberta's relations with the outside world.

Androgen is the male sex hormone, and the aura it projects, the insecurities it hides, the locker-room mentality it bolsters, explain the new rich kid on the block — the province of oil and cowboys and nouveau riche swagger. It is a strange province, aggressive in its new stance and surprisingly chippy toward outsiders. There is some question of whether it is willing to tolerate those areas of the country with differing cultural backgrounds.

Alberta is the male animal on display. The need to prove oneself in the primitive manner of a bull in rut makes the atmosphere of the place resemble an entire province posing for a hairy-chested after-shave lotion. There can be nothing more ludicrous than a grown man with a paunch teetering about Calgary on the high heels and pointed toes of embroidered cowboy boots, attempting to capture a reminder of some distant past. If the foot is a sex object, as a trendy new doctor claims, Alberta is abrim with eroticism.

These are man-boys playing in the make-believe world of their own playpen — exposed as pseudo-machismo caricatures only when they stray beyond their own borders. The costume parade — affected by otherwise normal businessmen — is, of course, a sham, because Alberta is not the stage for John Wayne it makes itself out to be. Since the Second World War, Canada has had the fastest urban growth rate of any country in the world, and Calgary is the fastest-growing city in the country.

It will be a fine city, as they say, when they finish uncrating it. Calgary has less green space per square foot in its downtown core than any city in Canada. In the race toward Mammon, green space got left behind. The skyline of the city is now a cardboard cutout, the towers reminiscent of the Metropolis backdrop for a Superman comic. The new towers make even more ridiculous the insane bulbous knob of the Calgary Tower, another example of the municipal fascination with such symbols that induced Toronto to add its own Disneyland touch to its view with its CN Tower.

The two towns perhaps have something in common — a lust for power and sway at the sacrifice of sensitivity. While Toronto is merely superior in its isolation, Calgary takes an aggressive stance against the rest of Canada. It was there, in this city famed for Western hospitality, in the professionally printed banners that hung in the Calgary Corral, the hockey rink, when Quebec Nordiques paid their first visit after the Calgary Cowboys' Rick Jodzio was suspended for his brutal attack on the Nordiques' top scorer Marc Tardif. The banners read: FROGS ARE BACK JUMPERS. Other signs in the arena showed the same delicate taste: JODZIO EATS FROGS and QUEBEC LES TURKEYS.

Somehow, there is the need to exert muscular dominance. Albertans do not pick and choose, they stampede. After enduring thirty-six straight years of sanctimonious rule under Social Credit, the electorate — one might have imagined — would have preferred some balance in the parliamentary system. Instead, they shy from providing an opposition that can be some check on government excess — they give Peter Lougheed's Tories seventy-three of the seventy-nine seats.

Albertans don't vote when they enter the polling booth as

much as they anoint. They don't cast ballots, they sprinkle water. The opposition is in effect composed of one member, the NDP's lonely Grant Notley. Two of every three Albertans vote the same way — an aberration in the political mosaic that makes up the rest of Canada. They are conformists with a vengeance — the only province that sends only one party to Ottawa. Twenty-one solid Conservatives.

Lougheed comes across as pensive on Joe Clark — who was once almost an office boy for him — saying the correct, necessary things as an executive would about a onetime junior.

No intellectual himself but a fiercely determined worker, Lougheed declined the opportunity to sit across the floor from Trudeau as leader of the Opposition. He did not even stay in the Ottawa Civic Arena for the final ballot of the Tory leadership contest in 1976. What his vote might have been is unknown, but all we know is that he didn't vote for Clark on the clinching ballot. He didn't vote for anyone.

There is one link with Quebec: the populations of the two precincts tend to veer toward uniformity of thought. They love landslides. If democracy is not entirely a frail flower in Alberta, the lack of opposition members does make for quite the dullest legislature in the country. It is an unusual week when Lougheed is asked an interesting question. For years, the cameras that televize the sittings were aimed at the government benches, capturing only the backs of the heads of the sparse opposition members. The general atmosphere is that of a nunnery at recess.

The mistake is to misjudge the province of rough faces and new wallets. Bruised pride is everything. When Premier Lougheed toured Europe in 1975, his entourage — including wives and press — totalled 110.

The mystique of the frontier male wafts over the province as thick as musk. There are few outstanding Alberta women who would come to mind for the average Canadian. There is not a single woman among the twenty-one MPs. The locker-room syndrome was most apparent among the tightly knit coterie of ex-athletes and thrusty success stories in Lougheed's first cabinets. A reporter observing them move like a phalanx around King Peter, as he was then known, at federal-provincial conferences always expected them to snap into a huddle and call the next play.

The base of it all, the folk rite that reveals the soul, is the anachronism called the Calgary Stampede, which every summer allows the abandoning of the frontier strictures that are in play the rest of the year. It is like some ancient Greek festival, when societal rules were set in abeyance for a set duration. Men who decline to swear in front of their secretaries are suddenly revealed as raunchy gropers who establish that the barriers are down in the after-office parties at the Calgary Inn (which I refuse to call The Westin). They treat women as they would a horse.

It is, in fact, the Canadian version of *Fasching*, the permissive celebrations of the flesh in Bavarian towns when the year's normal restrictions on conduct are abandoned. Stampede Week is when the Albertan climbs down out of his after-shave lotion ad and attempts to emulate the caricature. The boy-men are out of school.

Edmonton is more interesting than Calgary, a more livable city. The river valley of the North Saskatchewan that divides the town is one of the great assets of any Canadian city in winter and summer. But it is too cold. Brass monkeys change airline tickets just to avoid the place. It will become a less interesting town since the publisher of the *Edmonton Journal*, J. Patrick O'Callaghan, has just moved to take up the same post at the *Calgary Herald*. J. P. O'C. — as he's known to his staff — has been likened to a cannon loose on the deck of a frigate in a storm. With O'Callaghan and Ted Byfield in the same town at the same time the city may have to order more fire extinguishers.

Red Deer is the birthplace of Marjorie Nichols, the Victoria journalist, and one day it will erect a plaque in her honour. ("She doesn't have ulcers," it will say, "but she's a carrier.") When she starred in Ottawa as the Pearl Mesta of the journalistic set, she used to host parties to which she would invite Margaret but not Pierre. "He kills parties," she would explain. "They fall flat kerplunk on the floor when he arrives." She meant the social variety. Now he's killed the other variety.

Albertans, with their siege mentality, don't really mind the taunt that they have the only one-party government this side of Albania. They like less the suggestion that, to paraphrase Toynbee, Alberta may be the only jurisdiction in history that has gone from poverty to decadence without passing through civilization. Unlike the residents of Saskatchewan, who know their hearts are pure and God in Her socialist or Tory beneficence will take care of them, and unlike British Columbians, who simply don't give a damn, knowing golf is just around lunch, Albertans have a nonamused view of the rest of Canada, especially Ottawa, suspicious that the Eastern bastards want to steal their riches now that they've dug themselves out of Depression days.

One night in the Owl's Nest, the bar of the Calgary Inn, a visitor got up to say goodnight and tapped on the shoulder — as a method of saying farewell — one of the men seated around the table. A hand shot backward, an iron grip seized the visitor's arm, and he was warned, in threatening tones, that this "Eastern condescension" had gone on for too many years and Western grievances were going to be settled and on and on. Finally prising himself loose with some difficulty, the perplexed visitor — who happened to be from Vancouver — made his way to his bed. The chap issuing the threats turned out to be a transplant from Ontario. Marc Lalonde let loose a lot of hidden anger.

As a diplomat, he'd make a great piano-mover. With the province seething with rage over the effects of the National Energy Policy and the oil rigs heading south, the man who imported expensive oil from Venezuela for Eastern Canada while denying Alberta the world price for oil travelled to Cold Lake and Edmonton on a fence-mending tour in late January of 1981.

The trip was rare enough to make major news in Alberta, because the failure of the Liberal heavy hitters to show their faces in the province since their celebrated energy policy the previous October had further contributed to the anger. Lalonde, who has never lacked courage, was gaining points on his two-day tour until he came up with another of his gems.

Multinational oil companies always act strongly when

162

countries start to limit outside control over oil production, he said in an address to Alberta Indians. Then he thoughtfully added, "At least they have not brought the CIA in, like they did in certain foreign countries."

If there is an insult to be had, Lalonde will find it with the unerring gift of a water diviner. By giving the sly nudge that there might somehow be a connection with what went on in places such as Chile and what could go on in Alberta, Lalonde was playing for cheap applause before a minority group. That's a class act?

A University of Alberta professor's wife, who has lived in the United States, says there is a "whiff of Dallas" to the political air. She finds it chilling. J. O. Karpinka, president of Oleum Exploration Ltd., says in a letter to the *Calgary Herald* that the day the NEP was introduced, "budget day, Oct. 28, 1980, must rank as a day of infamy in this nation's history." He refers to that intrinsic emotion called freedom — "the very substance which people of our world are prepared to die for." One keeps running into references to death in conversations in Alberta this year. It is not a pleasant atmosphere.

Albertans, regarded as funny-money freaks by the outside world for those three and a half decades under the descendants of Bible Bill Aberhart, are further embittered by another factor. The lonely Tory toffs of the province have good reason for their frustration. For thirty-six years they wandered unappreciated outside the mainstream of Canadian political life as the mumbo-jumbo artists of Social Credit-ruled Alberta.

The leaders of the province were, in effect, regarded as lepers elsewhere in Canada. There was certainly no connecting bond of patronage with Ottawa. Then, a decade ago, there was a further waft of alienation when Alberta was a lonely island of capitalism in a sea of socialism, with the NDP controlling the governments of Manitoba, Saskatchewan and affluent British Columbia (the latter fact completely befuddling materialistic Albertans). The siege mentality and xenophobia simply increased. Earlier, when Peter Lougheed did his magnificent repair job on the provincial Conservative party, at least the nabobs of Calgary and Edmonton were plugged into one of the two major political parties — though they had to remain outside the federal trough as the Grits seemed destined to reign forever.

Then came Joe Clark. There's the basis of the further embitterment. Clark is not much respected in his home province, mainly because he can't ride a horse. In a culture that still retains the illusion that it is a cameo out of a Zane Grey novel, this apparently means a lot. Clark, admittedly, is one of the more uncoordinated specimens ever to tread the public stage.

He once confessed into my tape recorder in his office that the reason he can't swim has to do with a problem with his head. "It floats?" I asked in my famed suave manner. "No," he said, "I shouldn't tell *you* this, but it . . . um . . . *sinks*." At this his aide, Donald Doyle, who was seated behind him out of Clark's view, twisted his body into the fetal crouch and his lips formed a silent primordial scream, realizing what demons were to emerge later from my typewriter.

To this day, at my Saturday night parties when readings from *The Collected Wit of Herb Gray* pall and guests grow tired of my snapshot album showing the CNR double-tracked all the way from Larry Zolf's kosher log cabin in Winnipeg to the shores of the Pacific, I bring out my tape of Joe Clark explaining why his head is heavier than water.

But, to be fair — my constant weakness — there is a medical, or at least military diagnosis for Clark's coordination problems. I was walking with him one day and kept feeling as if I had three left feet, continually doing a quick shuffle, trying to keep in step. I finally realized why I could never do it. Most people, when they walk, move their left arm forward as their right foot goes forward — and vice versa.

Joe Clark, when he walks, swings his right arm forward with his right leg, his left arm with his left leg. He suffers from ambulatory dyslexia. I explained this discovery to my close buddy Marjorie Nichols, the *Vancouver Sun* columnist who regularly operates without anaesthetic on the politicians in the B.C. legislature. "That's right!" she cried. "If he'd been born a horse, he'd be a pacer!"

But, it must be explained, I said *most* people. Not everyone. The Canadian Army discovered the anomaly during the latest of our wars. There are some recruits, it found, who indeed cannot march in unison: they walk the way Clark does. The army has even devised a word for this. These incipient mercenaries are "zunters." That's now an official army word. So Joe Clark, when you puzzle over him on TV, is "zunting."

Mackenzie King, when you think of it, would never have survived in the age of television. Joe Clark, if present conditions prevail, has a good chance of being our next prime minister and, just as Mackenzie King was our first PM who talked with his dead mother and his dog, Clark was our first and (quite possibly) will be our second PM who zunts.

However, I digress. The advent of Clark in 1979 as prime minister (only one Alberta MP supported his leadership bid) at last promised to bring the lonely millionaires of Alberta into the national fold. It was fully expected that the decision-making bodies and all those nonelected boards in Ottawa would suddenly flower with these energetic and tough-minded Alberta men who had been denied their say for so long. The highest per capita income-earners in Canada being denied a role in running the country? It had been an unnatural state and was now to end.

There was talk of an Alberta figure heading the CBC and another getting a major position in the CNR. Once young Joe found the levers of power in Ottawa, it was expected (a natural expectation) that all those havens of patronage filled with fatted Liberals would be cleansed with lean-jawed Tories, a good percentage of them from Alberta.

Instead, as the violins whined and the rye turned to hemlock in the Petroleum Club, poor Clark and his Boy Amateurs did the kamikaze act in record time and the Albertans, just about to taste the national goodies, had them snatched away again.

It is sometimes hard to discern which is the strongest — the distaste for Pierre and the Reincarnates, or the contempt for the inability of Clark to accomplish what was expected of him. That is, a quick replacing of the movable bodies. The eminently fair and meticulous manner in which Clark's lady of patronage Jean Pigott, the Godmother, was sifting eager aspirants was subsequently viewed, in Alberta, as juvenile. The propertied class of Alberta bitterly saw itself shut out yet again for years ahead.

Considering its lonely existence for so long in the past, it was more understandable when there was a sudden spate of frustrated cries for a Western sovereign state unblemished by language promises and DREE grants. Pierre Trudeau's energy policies and constitutional obsessions certainly didn't help the situation, but at the base of the separatism mutterings was the anger (Tory anger at Tories, if you will) at seeing salvation so close, but then watching it slip away again.

Clark, sternly warning the prime minister from platform after platform that Western Canada is dangerously ripe for the separatist myth, passes on a mood that has gripped a certain small slice of Alberta society. But he must be nagged by the knowledge that he himself, by his ineptitude, unwittingly fanned the small flame.

If Clark is uncomfortable with his own province, Trudeau is mystified/indifferent by/to it. As a man who believes that his intellect can pierce steel plate at forty glances, Trudeau tends — when thwarted — to sulk and seek easier targets. This is the basis of his failures in Western Canada over fourteen years: being Number Two, he doesn't try harder.

This is even more peculiar because his principal advisers, over the period of his greatest failure have been from Alberta itself, the impenetrable castle. His brains have been steered by Ivan Head, Jimmy Coutts and Joyce Fairbairn, all Albertans who gravitated as adults to Ottawa and therefore would be presumed to be able to influence or educate a man who was past fifty before he spent much time west of Ottawa.

Head was a University of Alberta law professor who for ten years was Trudeau's heavy thinker and a writer of his more important speeches. He seems to have reserved his rented genius for global affairs, seldom casting his eye on Red Deer. Over the years he has had about as much influence on Trudeau's understanding of Western Canada as Wayne Gretzky has.

Joyce Fairbairn was a pert blond reporter from Alberta

who, with a well-turned ankle in the front row of press conferences in the miniskirt era, was often the subject of Trudeau's playful flirtations. She joined his office, and as his legislative assistant prepares him for the probable line of debate in question period every day. She is married to Michael Gillan, a former *Globe and Mail* reporter and saxophone player who has long been an executive assistant to Allan MacEachen. It is widely believed that Trudeau will place Fairbairn, forty-two, in the Senate before he departs his job. She does the verbal do-si-do when you mention it to her.

Coutts of course is an Alberta product, grew up there, took his law degree there and presumably would still have had some contacts in his home province that he could have passed on to the prime minister. It was Coutts and Fairbairn who convinced Trudeau to bribe Jack Horner to cross the floor, the worst political decision since Rudolf Hess parachuted into Scotland.

If there is anything the land of the cowboy detests it is a traitor, and lifetime Tory Horner, running as a Liberal, was trounced twice in Crowfoot by young Tory Arnold Malone, who is known around Ottawa as "Mortimer Snerd" from the Edgar Bergen days, because of his speaking style.

So Trudeau's main spokesmen to win the hearts and minds of Western Canadians were turncoats. Horner was a turncoat, Senator Argue, as we've seen, was a turncoat. Senator Olson was a turncoat. A Tory-turned-Liberal, a socialist-turned-Liberal, a Socred-turned-Liberal. It seems a strange way to build a political base. (The effectiveness of Senators Argue, Olson and Perrault, when they were the three senators in Trudeau's cabinet, can be judged by the fact that they were known as "Winken, Blinken and Nod" in their wanderings through this Liberal wasteland.)

The strange thing about Trudeau is that with his office full of Westerners, he still can't fathom the territory — and has given up trying. "I came to Ottawa to save Quebec," he told Joe Clark while discussing the transfer of power to the Tories after his 1979 defeat, "someone else is going to have to save the West."

167

His last three principal secretaries have been from the West: Austin from B.C., Coutts from Alberta, Axworthy from Manitoba. But none of the intelligence seems to take root.

It's not that there hasn't been *enough* advice. The fault lies in the receiving set. The sender was working. The receiver wasn't tuned in — or turned on.

A most important point that Trudeau and the panjandrums of Central Canada most dangerously ignore is that Alberta feels frustrated, trapped, the only province besides serene Saskatchewan without access to the sea. Alberta is a musclebound Switzerland. She aims to do something about it.

Peter Lougheed, a polite, pleasant man sits on a flowered couch in his huge office in Edmonton. He is free to admit that the reason he shocked his free enterprise friends by buying the Vancouver-based Pacific Western Airlines and moving it to Alberta is that his province will no longer abide being a prisoner of transportation systems controlled from afar. (Calgary is the only major city in Canada where the CPR lines still carve the downtown core like a Berlin Wall, forcing streets to duck under or rise above.)

As soon as the Supreme Court of Canada disagreed with Ottawa's objections and approved Alberta's PWA purchase, it was discovered the airline was talking merger with Transair, another line that sweeps across the northern prairie and into Toronto.

Now that Lougheed has his own airline, does he also want a route to the sea? He acknowledges the opening of the Mackenzie Valley corridor to the Arctic has been an Alberta (and family) dream since grandfather Sir James Lougheed advocated the project in the Senate. Some Albertans refer to Inuvik, in the Mackenzie delta, as "Alberta's port."

Mel Hurtig, the Edmonton publisher, used to say that there were more left-handed Mormon streakers in Western Canada than there were separatists. That's not quite true anymore, but there still aren't that many real live separatists out there. What you do have is a clutch of cowards.

A coward is someone who, faced with a fight, cuts and runs away. That is what a Western separatist is (Quebec is another question). Confronted with the need to work out an accommodation with the insular rulers of Ottawa, the separatist turns and runs, seeking thumb-sucking independence rather than a tiresome family quarrel. That's a coward.

Gordon Kesler, the Louis Riel of the bronco set, is not going to frighten any democracy. He went to a Utah college on a rodeo scholarship. (For those who keep track of items of the symbolism of certain classic movies, it should be recorded that one of the five children of Gordon Kesler is named Shane.) He makes his living as an oil patch spy using binoculars and contacts with oil rig workers to find out up-to-date drilling intelligence which he then sells to competing oil companies. It is common practice in the oil patch and, while not exactly illegal, certainly flirts in the unethical arena.

It is industrial espionage, in fact, a strange trade for a man calling for a new code of conduct in politics.

Olds-Didsbury, the riding that Kesler won for the Western Canada Concept (in Alberta, the Liberal party is now referred to as the "Eastern Canada Concept"), was the most susceptible seat in the province for his brand of Poujadism. It has never been represented by any of the old-line parties.

Always out there on the right-wing fringe, Olds-Didsbury was previously held for twenty-one years by now-retired Social Credit leader Bob Clark. A farming area halfway between Calgary and Edmonton — the town of Olds has eight grain elevators and now a waterbed store — the seat before going Socred was held by the United Farmers of Alberta. Any group of voters who feels that Peter Lougheed is too far to the *left* is breathing a special type of air denied most Canadians.

Kesler is so sophisticated that he told the microphones within minutes of being elected in February that "if we're lucky" Pierre Trudeau "will have a heart attack in the next five minutes."

Wiser minds convinced him to apologize for the remarks several days later, but at the WCC convention in July, some members displayed posters that said: COME WEST, TRUDEAU. They were decorated with a noose.

169

The voters in the Olds-Didsbury byelection went to the polls just after hearing about Westminster giving second-reading approval to Trudeau's new constitution which Kesler claimed would rob Albertans of property rights. Obviously a number of people believed him.

The fruitcake quality of the Alberta separatist movement can be judged by the fact that the man who founded it in 1975 is a lawyer from Victoria — which doesn't have to break away from Canada since it never joined it. Doug Christie has those evangelical eyes of an Elmer Gantry that burn like cigarette butts. He is in continual dispute with his Alberta brethren and is alternately tossed in and out of the WCC, in jurisdictional disputes that only a PTA meeting could admire. He fits Churchill's definition of a fanatic: someone who can't change his mind and won't change the subject.

Christie in fact is too pure-minded for the fuzzy philosophy of Kesler, who is now carefully trying to back away from the hard-core separatist band in the WCC, advocating that the voters would first be offered a referendum on the question. The bronco-buster adopts the tactics of the Quebec he would so like to shed.

Basically, it is the politics of cowardice. A Western Canada that survived the humiliation and the disasters of the Depression is now in the "have" haven in the provincial pecking order, loaded with resources, full of space and beckoning population. To advocate that the part of the country with the most potential of all should now cut and run is sad.

Separatists are sad, as are most cowards.

The essential problem is not separatism but Trudeau. What is taken for hatred of Ottawa is hatred of Trudeau. His confrontation style, his inability to work interestedly when he has no adversary, has poisoned the attitudes of those who think that in the Western Canada Concept lies their salvation. If Trudeau goes, Western separatism will disappear like a snowbank before a chinook.

14
British
Columbia
Narcissus-on-the-Pacific

Valium West has a quality all its own . . .
Victoria, God's waiting room . . .
voters weaned on kooks . . .
Wacky Bennett, or, Orson Welles lurching out
of a space bubble . . . Miniwac's menagerie . . .
the Grits as the last remnant of the class system . . .
Polynesian Paralysis

In the Maritimes, politics is a disease; in Quebec a religion; in Ontario a business; on the Prairies a cause. In British Columbia? Entertainment.

Angus MacInnis, legendary CCF figure

We are now in British California. Bennett Columbia. Home of Social Credit and the Sasquatch (the Sasquatches are the ones with the *big* feet). Those in the Bill Bennett cabinet who are not millionaires are car dealers. In fact, there's a rumour that the entire province is going to be put on a two-year, 50,000-mile warranty.

Valium West has a quality all its own. It was the most affluent jurisdiction in the world ever to democratically elect a socialist government when it chose the NDP to govern it in 1972. The new premier, Dave Barrett, was forty-three years of age and took office having never been to Montreal in his life. The first Jewish premier in Canadian political history had been to Seattle, where he studied under the Jesuits, and he had been to St. Louis, where he went to graduate school and became an adoring expert on Franklin Delano Roosevelt. But he had never been to Montreal. It is our ignorance that binds our country together.

To understand B.C. politics (millions of Canadians would rather not try), one must understand that the province was run for twenty years by a man named Wacky Bennett who had as his most popular minister the Rev. Phlying Phil Gaglardi while Vancouver was administered by Mayor Tom Terrific Campbell. To be a politician in B.C., one must tap-dance, juggle and, if necessary, drop one's pants.

This is in large part because Victoria, God's Waiting Room, is the only capital in the country that is physically detached from the vast majority of the people it governs. (Ottawa is detached mentally.) The result of this is that there is the constant sense of being afloat. Stern mothers, who knew what they were doing from their own experience, used to advise their daughters never to go to a party on a yacht. There is a detachment from reality, with subsequent consequences. Victoria can be described as Political Love Boat. Some of the characters are interchangeable.

It was no real surprise that within a year of Barrett taking power, a cabinet minister had to be sacked for being caught *in flagrante delicto* in a car within a fifty-yard view of the premier's office window. Or that the social hostess of the stately Empress Hotel complained about two NDP ministers, installed in a suite close by the one reserved for Prince Philip, who were cooking their meals by hotplate and leaving the beer bottles rolling about the Persian carpet. Or the Social Credit lady MLA who had to request that the Empress management switch her room because of the steady tattoo of passion exerted on the wallboards of the adjoining room due to the amorous nightly adventures of one particularly randy NDP minister.

All of this is in keeping with the great traditions of B.C. politics. Voters in the nethermost province have been weaned on kooks, from the day more than a hundred years ago when an itinerant from the California goldfields, one William Smith, felt his name was too commonplace. He changed it to Amor de Cosmos — lover of the universe — became B.C.'s second premier and once delivered a speech lasting seven hours. He founded the *Victoria Colonist*, the oldest newspaper on the entire North American Pacific coast (now put into a bastard merger with the *Victoria Times* by the money-squeezing Thomson owners). A bizarre and eccentric character, he sat for a while in the House of Commons and in his last speech there expressed the view — extremely advanced for the time — that Canada should have the power to negotiate her own commercial treaties.

174

Down through the years, the longing for slightly deranged statesmen has persisted. One of W. A. C. Bennett's ministers, who now earns his living as a piano-tuner, became the first minister in Commonwealth history to be sent to jail for accepting bribes, most of which he spent on indifferent rugs and tacky furniture.

There was the famed Socred MLA Lydia Arsens, who fought fluoridation and once proposed to the legislature that all householders be required to have three garbage cans, in three colours, to make life easy for the dustman — since the red can would contain tins, the white one waste paper and the blue one such mundane things as coffee grounds and soggy tea bags.

It didn't quite rank, really, with the crowd-pleasing antics of Phlying Phil, the evangelical speed freak who saved thousands of souls in his Kamloops Sunday School empire in splendiferous Oral Roberts fervor while also roaming the continent in government jets, sometimes neglecting to remember who was paying for it. While upholding the law as B.C. highways minister, he was convicted of speeding and careless driving offenses, had his driver's licence suspended, was fined $1,000 for contempt of court and once sped away after running over a dog, only to be overtaken by an irate motorist — and voter.

The Reverend Gaglardi, in a passionate plea for understanding, one day cried in the legislature, "If I tell a lie it's only because I think I'm telling the truth!"

There was Wacky Bennett himself, an abstemious teetotaler who dressed in a black homburg and a funeral director's suit, roamed the province in a black limousine, zoomed around the mountain passes and descended on small towns rather like Orson Welles lurching out of a space bubble.

In some perverse way, he collected around him a technicolor retinue of flacks, touts, rounders and sycophants. They reeked of hair oil and loud socks, chain-smokers who furtively hid in the end car on the premier's train, drinking rye late at night like boys behind the barn, hiding out from the boss who sedately played bridge up ahead with his constant companion, a terrible-tempered minister named Waldo Skillings who once hit a female Conservative opponent during a radio debate and had a habit of falling up the down escalators.

One of Bennett's retainers — all of whom looked as if they'd failed the early auditions for *Guys and Dolls* — went to jail for forging the premier's signature on a letter to the prime minister's office; another used his name to call phony press conferences for mining promoters and a third wrote a fawning book on Bennett that was so dreadful it almost won, unentered, the Stephen Leacock Medal for Humour.

Wacky's successor, Dave Barrett, regularly saved voters from wasting their time watching *Hee Haw*. On stage, he was something fit only for a home movie: wrenching off his jacket, his tie, on occasion even his shoes. Short, fat, profane — a socialist Buddy Hackett — he had John Diefenbaker's timing crossed with Lenny Bruce's vocabulary.

He consumed Chinese food by the bushel, travelled to Japan to play on his Old-Timers rugby team (where he was in constant danger of losing his pants) — and lasted only three years in office.

The probable turning point was when he rounded a corner outside the legislative chamber one day and spotted columnist Marjorie Nichols, who had been savaging him in her usual surgical way and at the time was chatting with his executive assistant. "Fuck you! Fuck you! Fuck you!" screamed Dave Barrett.

Ms. Nichols, who had heard the word before, began her column the next day: "A short rotund man in a blue suit approached me in a corridor of the B.C. Legislature yesterday. I recognized him immediately as the premier of British Columbia, because he was shouting..." Mr. Barrett never really recovered politically after that.

The B.C. demand for balminess affects even those hired to represent the Queen's dignity. Speaker Gordon Dowding, an NDP lawyer, got into a row in the House after it was revealed he used the legislative dining room to cater a private party and the telltale cherry tomatoes were sprinkled down the legislative steps. Premier Barrett, watching the robed Dowding march stiffly down the corridor in his tricorne, cracked, "I think the job has gone to his three-cornered head."

176

Barrett's attorney-general, Alex Macdonald, in kilt and sporran, played tennis with Bobby Riggs on the Empress lawn, doing a striptease throughout until he emerged in his shorts. The powerful doctrinaire socialist, Resources Minister Bob Williams, used to reply to reporters' tough questions by smiling sweetly and saying: "Kiss my ass, daddy."

There was the celebrated Agnes Kripps, a gushing Socred of yellow coiffure who one day aroused snoozing MLAs with an earnest speech explaining that there were too many sniggers about the word "sex," it was embarrassing to children and that she proposed replacing it with an entirely new word — bolt — for Biology of Living Today.

There was a thunderous clatter as MLAs of all parties sat up with a start. "I'm bolt upright just listening to you," cried an NDP backbencher. As poor, flustered Mrs. Kripps tried to flounder on, a Socred shouted, "It's okay for the bolts, but what about the nuts?"

Mrs. Kripps, refusing to quit when she was behind, finally attempted to silence the hilarity all about her by pleading to the chair: "Mr. Speaker! Mr. Speaker! Won't you please bang that thing of yours on the table!"

Today's legislature has some of the same characteristics that have made B.C. politics so justifiably renowned from sea to shining sea. Mr. Bennett's majority is down to three seats, the Speaker has had a heart bypass operation, another member is on a pacemaker and the Socred government whip, who is seventy-four, has been cited as the correspondent in a divorce case involving adultery in the back seat of a white Cadillac convertible. (You think I'm making this up, but this is British California.)

As a result, the fate of the Bennett government rests not so much on politics as on the medical profession. Considering the government's most recent war with doctors over fees, I'd hate to be the first Socred cabinet minister who enters hospital for an appendectomy. He may emerge with a vasectomy.

Beside all this, the premier, a card-carrying workaholic, finds it rather hard to compete. He is unique in the Commonwealth, certainly in Canada, part of a unique father-son act that had the senior Bennett premier for twenty years and now his son heading into his eighth year in the same role. They are different, of course. For one thing, when Bill Bennett goes from Vancouver to the legislature in Victoria, he takes the ferry. His father used to walk.

Bill Bennett is energetic, alert, rich, dedicated — all those things that moved journalist Christina Newman, after two hours with him, to conclude that he had "a relentless dullness" and was "eminently forgettable." Another female reporter, in the midst of a TV profile designed to reveal the real man behind the political mask, in frustration demanded, "Don't you ever *indulge* yourself in anything?"

"Well, yes," replied Miniwac solemnly, "peanut butter sandwiches." He held his fingers apart before the camera to indicate the sinful thickness of the crime.

He cannot compete with his underlings, who speckle his pristine image with juvenile excesses, like Fuller brush salesmen given their first out-of-town trip with a credit card. Consumer Affairs Minister Peter Hyndman, champion of the downtrodden, is detected charging $374.57 for a dinner for six, including four bottles of $37.50 Pouilly-Fuisse, and is deposed. Labour Minister Bob McClelland is detected with a $1,298 New York expense account, including $325 for tickets to *Sugar Babies*, the raunchy Mickey Rooney burlesque musical. Finance Minister Hugh Curtis, at a time when Bennett is preaching restraint to the unwashed, has his records reveal $1,200 on Broadway tickets that include a research trip to *The Best Little Whorehouse in Texas*. W. A. C. Bennett groans in his grave and turns on his side.

The reason why you must entertain British Columbians before they will listen to your philosophy is that they are hedonists. They enjoy the best quality of life, which is different from (i.e., better than) the best standard of living in Canada — which means in the world. Industrialists moan about B.C. having the highest hourly wages in North America, about the boy spraying lettuce in the Vancouver supermarket for twelve dollars an hour, the woman slicing pies on the B.C. ferries who makes fourteen dollars an hour.

British Columbians, with the highest percentage of unionized workers on the continent (the possible exception being coal-mining West Virginia), feel there is nothing wrong with this. Since this is the best place in the cosmos to live, why should not the wages be the highest?

Residents of B.C. in fact have achieved the ultimate of the consumer/acquisitive society as preached nightly on colour TV. There is a fuzzing over of class lines, and plumbers, butchers and piano-movers — obeying what they are taught by TV and magazine ads — feel they deserve the same sailboats, ski cabins and cantilevered waterfront homes as doctors, lawyers and stockbrokers. This is distinctive B.C. logic: to prove that there is a classless society, there must be strikes all the time, those on strike demonstrating that their monthly payments on the boat are just as onerous as those paid by their dentist. It is not so much the revolution of the blue collar as what could be called the osmosis creep. There's the Shaughnessy Heights story of the man whose sink plugged up on a Sunday night so he had to call a plumber. The workman stayed fifteen minutes and charged seventy-five dollars.

The householder exploded. "Look," he fumed, "I'm a lawyer and even I couldn't charge those rates."

"Oh, I know," sympathized the plumber. "Neither could I when I was a lawyer."

The reason the Liberals disappeared in B.C. is that they defied this rule. They were the last remnants of the class system. The federal Liberals drew their guidance from that table in the Vancouver Club ruled over by Senator deB. Farris. Patronage flowed to the selected law firms, and the masters of the party failed to notice that the province was becoming filled up with newcomers from the Prairies who owed their allegiance to protest parties called NDP and Social Credit.

The provincial wing of the party, with its upper middle class tastes, became hived into the silk stocking ridings in Vancouver and Victoria that had yacht clubs and tennis clubs. If a child had braces on its teeth, you could bet its father was a Liberal. It became not so much a political party as a cocktail party.

The small coterie of provincial Liberal MLAs were cut from such a mould (out of *Esquire*, wives by Junior League) that they began to resemble the *Sports Illustrated* Silver Anniversary All-American basketball team. One of them, Allan Williams, was so dignified it was said that he fell down one day and broke his suit. It was suspected he slept in a Birks box.

Mr. Williams today is B.C.'s attorney-general, eventually leaping (after years of denials) with his silver-haired mates at the standing offer of top cabinet posts in Miniwac's Socred government. This act of philosophical consistency, of course, endeared the Liberal party further in the eyes of local voters.

The only one who refused to succumb to the bribes was Gordon Gibson, son of a millionaire, once the provincial leader, three times an unsuccessful federal candidate, formerly the most bushy-tailed Liberal cheerleader in the province.

Gibson, as a political aide in Ottawa in 1967, was one of the very first men to put together the organization that convinced Pierre Trudeau to run for the leadership. He worked in the PM's office, was close to him, in fact, was the trusted one chosen to drive Trudeau to his secret wedding.

Today Gibson is so livid at what federal policies and indifference have done to Liberal fortunes in B.C. that he has publicly denounced the government and refused to attend the celebrated fund-raising dinner at which Trudeau lectured Vancouverites on their inability to climb their own mountains. Gibson and a small group of supporters toyed with the idea this spring of Gibson openly declaring himself a contender for the Liberal leadership as a champion of Western Canadian interests — a race he never could have won but which would have been designed to smoke out Trudeau and make him declare more clearly his resignation timetable.

An example of the Gibson disillusionment with the blind masters of obfuscation in Ottawa was the delightful scam known as the Canada Development Corporation.

When Gibson still had some influence with the prime minister, he convinced him of the necessity of giving the West some sense of having a say in some of the national decision-making bodies — especially in the financial field. (This was in the era a decade ago when the Trudeaucrats marched out to Calgary for the much-trumpeted Western Economic Opportunities Conference. When it was over an irritated Trudeau, buffeted by Western premiers, muttered that this was the first "and last" such conference. It was.)

There was a great thunder of headlines in Vancouver papers when Ottawa announced that the CDC, son of Walter Gordon, would have its headquarters established in The Village on the Edge of the Rain Forest. Gibson beamed. Ottawa was sincere about decentralization.

There was just one problem, it turned out. CDC president Tony Hampson, a good Eastern product, didn't want to live in Vancouver. He preferred to stay in Toronto, close to the Ottawa mothership.

The CDC opened its "head office" in Vancouver in the most expensive property, high in a waterfront tower with the best view in town of the harbour and mountains, filled it with the right art and furniture — while Hampson collected *his* staff around him in Toronto.

On his token trips to Vancouver, hammered by reporters at press conferences, I used to greet him with, "Welcome to Vancouver, Mr. Hampson. Find your way in from the airport okay?"

Eventually, to cover its embarrassment, the CDC hired a retired Vancouver banker, John Ellis, as "chairman" — to give the castrated head office that wasn't a head office some supposed clout.

When those of us who are paid to do such things continued to heap abuse on the fraud, the CDC next hired a Vancouver-based public relations man. *Wonderful!* When you're not telling the truth in the first place, hire a flack. The poor shill was assigned to convince the locals that while the president and his operating officers remained in Toronto, running the show, the collection of secretaries and nonentities cluttering up the exquisite offices overlooking the sea was really the head office after all. It was a typical Liberal operation, like the storefronts in a Hollywood horse opera, all sham, no backup.

Still a favourite tale is the time the directors of the CDC

forced the local directors into a 7:00 AM board meeting so they could catch the great silver bird back to Toronto without disturbing their body clocks.

Early in 1981, on a Friday the thirteenth, Ellis as token chairman was replaced by Winnipeg industrialist Frederick W. Sellers. Less than three months later, the Trudeaucrats decided to make a move on the Winnipegger who had replaced a Vancouverite on the Vancouver-based $3.4 billion operation that was run from Toronto.

Their choice was the celebrated Maurice Strong (an abortive Liberal candidate in Toronto) who confessed that Finance Minister Allan MacEachen (since bounced into External Affairs) had offered him the job.

The astonishing attempted putsch was beaten back at the annual meeting after the press revealed the sly plot. But the federal craniums, trying to win the West, got their way. They placed on the board such as Paul Martin, Jr., the Montreal shipping executive who allows that he will be into Liberal politics in time, and Halifax lawyer William Mingo, a member of the Liberal federal executive, recruited for the CDC by MacEachen.

They joined such as Mary Lamontagne, who happens to be the wife of Defence Minister Maurice Lamontagne. When the little coup was finished, it meant that only two of the twenty-one directors (including Sellers) were from the West. It meant that all three Vancouver representatives were off the board, leaving Vancouver, where the CDC was supposedly based, without a voice in the body.

Even this outrage finally penetrated the bunker in Ottawa and, four months later, there was a shamefaced shuffle. Two Vancouver Liberal bodies were airlifted aboard: a mining executive and — surprise! — former cabinet minister Bob Andras.

In June of 1982, of course, it was announced that the CDC was to be sold off, loosed from denmother Ottawa. It was the culmination of Liberal hypocrisy: the federal government did not have either the guts to move it to the Toronto money markets where it probably belonged in the first place, or the courage to admit to Vancouver that it was all fakery. So endeth the lesson.

There are varying theories, of course, as to why the inhabitants of Narcissus-on-the-Pacific are so different from the rest of dull Canadians. There is the belief that Polynesian Paralysis, the *mañana* disease, comes with the Pacific currents and induces executives into hot-tubs when they should be knee-deep in accounts.

There is the theory, also, that the dregs of humanity drift to the edge of the frontier and, being unable to swim to Japan, stay to interbreed and multiply.

The real difference, it has come to me, is that people in British Columbia don't wear hats.

Each month as I migrate between Upper Canada and the Lotus Eaters, my system clogged with Air Canada toy food, I am left with a puzzled air, a culture-shocked refugee who finds something slightly uneasy about street scenes, something slightly off-key.

It suddenly became apparent the other day. No one in Vancouver wears headgear. When you retreat from an Ottawa or Montreal where the locals must protect their ears as they would their jewels, the sight of all these bare heads open to the elements portends a strange new tribe. British Columbians go through life from womb to tomb without ever putting anything on their headbone, a circumstance that leads to differences as well as luxuriant natural fur on top.

Outsiders would claim that this ability to exist without a cranium blanket merely accounts for the fact that the brain in B.C. has a convertible roof and simply leaks out the top. This, they claim, accounts for the production of politicians who go by such aforementioned names as Wacky, Phlying Phil and Tom Terrific.

This has nothing to do with it. British Columbians simply insist — since they have to put up with politicians — that they be entertainers also. (Was not Churchill a great entertainer, i.e., performer? JFK? Hitler? Fiorello La Guardia? Trudeau? Dief? It's the reason Joe Clark has such a struggle: he can't entertain.) W. A. C. Bennett, in fact, wore a homburg, and one of the reasons he stayed in power for twenty years is that he was the only B.C. citizen most voters had ever seen who wore a hat. They assumed it was a crown.

One of the reasons John Kennedy was elected president was that he never wore a hat. Since most people look ridiculous in hats, he reasoned that he would eliminate the possibilities of being photographed in one.

Americans recognized in JFK a free spirit (as subsequent revelations have proven). If he'd been a Canadian, he would have been a British Columbian, possibly almost as popular as Tom Terrific Campbell, the Vancouver mayor who didn't even go into a phone booth to don his cape and beat up hippies.

The hatless state accounts for the suspicion and mistrust that the natives have for their blood brothers who dwell across the mountains. Every night, British Columbians sit before their television sets, puzzling at the strange scenes before them out of Ottawa and way points, all those people marching about the streets with their creative juices wrapped in stifling headgear.

It is somewhat like watching a ritual out of Pago Pago, people who don't dress like *real* Canadians, i.e., British Columbians. They dress *funny*. Can they really be fellow citizens to be trusted?

People in Vancouver, mostly women, do carry protective devices over their heads when out in the open, to ward off the dew, but they are folded and shucked once indoors. There isn't a single woman in the province who knows how to wear a hat, where it goes or what it is supposed to protect. It's why they look so out of place once they have to venture out of civilization to other portions of the Dominion.

Men in B.C. regard umbrellas essentially as they do abortion: they don't think about it and don't want to get involved.

The result of all this hatlessness is that the inhabitants are different from the rest of Canadians. The breezes blowing over their naked scalps stimulate both the left and the right portions of the brain, making it all loosey-goosey and amenable to exotic strains (i.e., Social Credit) and forbidden fruits (i.e., tennis in December) denied to their earmuffed cousins.

One feels more free when one has reached the age of forty without ever owning a pair of gloves or a single hat. It is

184

liberating and puts one in concert with nature. Thoreau could explain it (and get elected here).

There are the Boat People and the Village People and the Displaced People. If you wish to understand B.C. (not everyone wishes to), think of it as the home of the Hatless People and everything will come clear.

15
Fourth Stopover

*The Village on the Edge
of the Rain Forest*

Vancouver: the worst weather in the world
and the best climate . . . downtown martini-land
to complete wilderness in twenty minutes . . .
the last retreat of hot-line shows . . .
the mouth that roared . . .
home again

Vancouver is the hot-tub and waterbed concession of the land, the Canadian equivalent of the Italian economy: nothing seems to work but everyone is contented, heading for the water. Vancouver is unreal, as unreal a microcosm of Canada as Ottawa is unreal, but it's a good slap in the face after a spell in the capital. It's as useful as shock treatment. An alternative to the yin and yang might be Sudbury. But I've been to Sudbury.

Vancouver is like London. It has the worst weather in the world and the best climate. There is a difference. Ottawa, the most unfortunately situated capital of any allegedly advanced country, has two wretched seasons, relieved only by a delightful autumn that can last up to forty-three days and some minutes, and a spring that sometimes can consume ninety-six hours. Its residents cower, from birth, before Mother Nature. Vancouverites pat her on the head and paddle off.

People who gravitate to Vancouver are essentially simple people in that they do not like bother. They do not like the bother, the fuss, of having to own two wardrobes. All you need in Vancouver is a light raincoat, a strong ego and $40,000 a year so as to stay above the basic poverty level.

At any party in Upper Canada, the chap standing about with a puzzled expression on his puss is a B.C. refugee, watching the elaborate fifteen-minute ritual of removing galoshes, scarves, mufflers, mitts, overcoats, hats, earmuffs and frost-free clavicle-protectors. By the time you do this at the start of the evening and then have to prepare for the same ritual at leaving, there's hardly time left in the evening to discuss the charisma of Sinclair Stevens.

Basically, there's the difference. Vancouverites are cowards when it comes to discomfort. We are only here three score and ten. It has always mystified me, for example, why millions of people suffering from the shilling gas meter and bone-searching chill, live in Liverpool and Manchester when they could be in Alicante or Sorrento.

Vancouver people feel the same way. They are not provincial. They are merely content. Newscasts about Eastern Canadian blizzards are ignored. They are not interested in anyone who does not share their hedonism. To be truthful, they view other Canadians with an air of amused pity.

This is the reason why British Columbia has never provided a prime minister. The wives won't allow it. The brightest and best in B.C. — those lawyers with strong jaws, silvered temples, golden tonsils and a good squash racquet — never run for federal office because their wives can read. They read the Ottawa weather report in the newspaper and, zap, there goes the political career.

The Cardiac Special (the overnight Air Canada flight from Vancouver to Ottawa) has ruined more marriages than the pro at the golf club. It takes little devotion to the nation to be a member of the Tuesday-to-Thursday Club — those Quebec and Ontario MPs who get an early start and a late arrival on their weekends. (On some Mondays the Tory ranks in the Commons resemble Dresden, circa 1945 and you could lob a watermelon into the Grit backbenches and not splatter one of those rural Quebec ties that look as if they had been purchased at the wallpaper store.) It takes rather more devotion to live three time zones away in Narcissus-on-the-Pacific — that's a lot of dogfood — and attempt to fly home every other weekend to acquaint your constituents with the latest arithmetical wizardry of Allan MacEachen's boffins, who somehow turned a $10 billion deficit into a $20 billion deficit.

190

That's why B.C. never has dominant cabinet ministers, when it has any. All the smart chaps are on their yachts, their ski slopes, or in their hot-tubs. (Their wives are with the golf club pro.) None of them is in Ottawa.

The main point about Vancouver is that it is probably the largest city in the world so close to immediate wilderness. This was pointed out some fifteen years ago by the *New York Times* in a most telling incident when two foolish Sunday afternoon hikers on a North Shore mountain in winter ventured beyond the limits of their endurance and daylight. Dressed in light clothes as darkness and rain closed in, they grew exhausted, confused and finally panicky.

Stumbling down a mountain stream, they lost their shoes; one sprained his ankle so badly he couldn't walk and the other left him huddled under a stump and somehow found his way down the mountain.

For days, in the pelting rain and chilling nights, just above suburban split-level range on the mountain, searchers combed the slopes for the crippled and unhappy hiker. The *Times*, in a front-page passage, tried to explain this inconceivable picture to its teeming masses: how the trapped man could look down on the lights of a modern city, with rescuers only thirty minutes away, but still be held in the grip of complete wilderness — before finally being rescued.

It's true. You can get more quickly into the primeval forest than in any city anywhere — from downtown martini-land in twenty minutes (quicker if you've had two). You can cross the Lions Gate Bridge to the North Shore mountains and — if it were possible — walk straight to the North Pole with the strong possibility that you would never encounter another human being on the way.

That sort of sense tends to do something to you. It doesn't tend to make you want to become prime minister.

In the elevator leading to the famous Top of the Mark bar in the Mark Hopkins Hotel in San Francisco — the best view in that most civilized of American cities — there is a sign that states there are six spectacular cities in the world. They are listed, in no particular order: Hong Kong, Rio de Janeiro, San Francisco, Sydney, Vancouver, Cape Town.

Of the six, I have yet to see Rio but will concede it number one spot on track record and on what I have seen and heard of it from afar.

Of the others, Vancouver is certainly number two or three.

San Francisco, for all its soft pastel beauty and undulating hills, lacks the truly arresting geographical features. Sydney, too, for all the beauty of its winding harbour and the architectural shock of that billowing-sails opera house, has the absence of a sharp vertical lift in a visual sense.

Hong Kong is the reverse of Vancouver, the residential side on the flat and the throbbing financial-hotel section across the water on Victoria Peak which rises as sharply as Vancouver's mountains — its exotic colours and vibrant millions perhaps exaggerating its geographical gifts.

Cape Town, ignored in the purdah of South Africa's current rank in world opinion, is so stunning with the looming presence of Table Mountain and its remarkably groomed leafy drives that it ranks with Hong Kong as a legitimate competitor to Vancouver, which is a babe among its rivals.

So what we have here is one of the three most beautiful cities in the world in the realm of physical setting. It is one of the two cities of the globe (Beirut is the other) where the skiers can look down on the bikinis and, at a certain selected time in the spring, switch places.

Inside the skin of The Village on the Edge of the Rain Forest there is, ahem, another animal.

All this beautiful scenery does, however, make for some interesting logistical challenges. Everywhere you go in Vancouver you have to get on a bridge to get somewhere else. The downtown core is in effect an island, with five of the six accesses to it by bridge or viaduct. This naturally shapes the traffic routes, the traffic mentality and, eventually, the *personality* of the city. One of the newspaper chains recently decided against establishing a third paper in Vancouver because its research showed a community chopped up by water, creating pockets of tinier communities rather than a homogeneous whole.

In Vancouver, everyone hates everyone else. The unions

hate management. The teachers hate the government. The government hates the doctors. Those who wear bathing suits at the beach hate those who refuse to wear anything. City council fights with Victoria which fights with Ottawa. It's why foreign wars and disasters sometimes have trouble making the front page of the local papers; there's so much local blood.

Fiery radicals bent on class warfare dominate city council in a place that has the easiest lifestyle in the country. The polls are topped each election by Alderman Harry Rankin, a rumpled Marxist who can hurl eloquent insults at an opponent for fifteen minutes without once repeating himself. Because of his politics, the Vancouver Bar Association attempted to prevent him from practising his calling when he graduated from the University of B.C. law school — even though he had just come back from fighting a war for Canada. A second alderman, Bruce Yorke, is a Communist black sheep from a wealthy Vancouver family. A third, a reformed alcoholic, terrorizes Skid Road hotels where, like Carrie Nation, he preaches against the Demon Rum and harasses them into cleaning up their act. He knows their tables. He used to sleep under them.

The mayor, Mike Harcourt, is a thirty-nine-year-old socialist lawyer who lives on the trendiest townhouse street, which overlooks False Creek and the mountains and is due for a beautification scheme — after a civic election is safely out of the way.

Because of all this verbal violence, Vancouver is the last retreat of hot-line shows, otherwise known as open-mouth radio. The airwaves tingle with the cries of the wounded, and politicians regularly carry on their wars via the wireless, shouting down old age pensioners and the unemployed. It's a day-long circus of the tonsils.

As proof of the seriousness of the game, last year the Hon. Rafe Mair, B.C.'s minister of health, shucked his cabinet post for the delights of becoming a hot-line host on a Vancouver radio station. If this would appear strange, we should only remind ourselves of the growing link between politics and show biz.

There is a new shortcut between the two provided by

those to the south of us. Since the most successful politicians are those who can become supreme actors in public, the Americans in their practical way have eliminated one step in the process by electing an actor. No learning process is required. Ronnie Reagan can dimple and prevaricate and obfuscate without any apprenticeship, a born bluffer right out of the starting gate. The crossbreeding between politicians and entertainers is stepping up, complete with fuzzification of the line dividing bafflegab and bubble gum.

Just as California leads the Excited States of America in innovation, so too does B.C. in Canada. To understand the political nuances you must realize that Mr. Mair, in his decision to promote himself from the public interest to the esoteric heights of open mouthery, replaced host John Reynolds, who himself plunged into radio because he felt his previous role — serving the public as a member of Joe Clark's caucus — was not commensurate with his talents (and he therefore grabbed a mike instead).

Premier Bennett, retaliating swiftly, filled Mr. Mair's post of health minister with the duck-tailed Jim Nielsen who (you've got to follow this closely) was a former hot-line host on the same station that recycled Mr. Reynolds, a Tory, in favor of Mr. Mair, a former Liberal who is now Social Credit. The same station, to demonstrate its ecumenical nature, nearly lured former premier Dave Barrett out of politics with a $100,000 offer to vent his tonsils for the greater good of advertisers rather than waste them on deaf public ears.

In all, this is an admirable trend, proof incarnate that the trade of politics is a sort of kindergarten course on the way to the riches of the marketplace, a way station on the path to true stardom which, as we all know, involves presiding at the opening of new service stations on Saturday afternoons. (Ronnie, having proven his credentials as a shill for General Electric and 20 Mule Team borax cleanser on TV before entering politics, thereby demonstrated that he understood the basis of politics.)

Rafe Mair, who practised law for years and did well in real estate, for some time was B.C.'s minister in charge of federal-provincial relations and travelled to London and Europe on the tortuous path to a new constitution. By decreeing that there is a higher calling still, answering housewives' complaints and lecturing electronically, he has given us all a lesson in priorities political.

It should come as no surprise, this crossover between earnest good works and dollar-a-holler radio. The federal minister of sport, Gerry Regan, was a sports announcer before he was premier of Nova Scotia. Jim Fleming, the Liberals' minister of propaganda and ethnic advertising boondoggling, is a Toronto radio product. Don Jamieson, the famed Golden Pipes, baffled his gab on behalf of Newfoundland private radio before inflicting it on puzzled foreigners as Canada's external affairs minister. Geoff Scott, a Hamilton Tory MP and high school friend of Rich Little, was celebrated when a TV reporter in the Press Gallery for his devastating imitations of Robert Stanfield and Joe Clark — a gift that has now strangely disappeared from his repertoire. Chuck Cook, an invisible Tory MP from North Vancouver-Burnaby, was an open-mouth host on that same Vancouver station that acts as a farm team for politicians who are either rising or falling on their luck.

The reason B.C. broadcasters want to be politicians (and vice versa) is that they all wallow in the slipstream of The Mouth That Roared, Jack Webster, a superb journalist who inherited the ham of Harry Lauder and now makes some $300,000 annually with five months off. Blather McHaggis has been in the country for thirty-five years but every time he gets a raise his accent gets thicker. If his income increases any more, he'll be speaking Croatian. He is truly B.C.'s ombudsman because of the clout of his radio hot-line show, which he has now moved to television. He has been nominated for an honorary degree from Simon Fraser University in honour of his gifts, plans to entitle his memoirs *Bullshit is My Business* and regularly refuses overtures from all political parties on the grounds that he can't afford the demotion to either his wallet or his power.

The rewards in this crazy field are such that some grow greedy. Before the late Judy LaMarsh became a Vancouver radio host, she was sued for libel by Ed Murphy, a testy broadcaster who this year was sent to jail for conspiring to offer a $100,000 bribe to a Social Credit cabinet minister who turned out to be the aforementioned Mr. Nielsen who has succeeded Mr. Mair who succeeded Mr. Reynolds.

All of them pale into insignificance before the late Rene Castellani, a promotion manager for the most successful Vancouver station, who set out on a marathon flagpole sitting stunt on behalf of the station's favourite charity. The only problem was that Castellani had a habit, after dark, of sneaking down the pole and, on the way to his girl friend's, visiting his ailing wife in hospital where he fed her milkshakes laced with arsenic. Sent up the river for murder, he spent his weekends playing drums in the prison band which called itself The Hangman's Five. Ronnie Reagan has a lot to answer for. . . .

The best way to detect the new fabric of the town is to glance at the graduation pictures of one of the city's tonier private girls' school, where faces from well-fixed Hong Kong and Southeast Asian families make up half the class. The reason Vancouver has the highest real estate prices in the country is that it is the home of the good life, the most comfortable spot in Canada to live. With the British lease on the crown colony of Hong Kong running out in 1997, money is being tucked safely into B.C. properties. Bob Lee, one Vancouver real estate salesman, has become a millionaire by selling off most of downtown Vancouver to Hong Kong and Southeast Asian money. One would not be surprised to see Stanley Park go next.

The Vancouver newspapers have some of the oldest staffs in the country, defying the usual vagabond nature of the trade, simply because the living is so pleasant that the vagabonds, once discovering Valhalla, refuse to move on. There is nowhere near the flux there is in papers in, say, Toronto. Publishers moan about this, while heading for the golf course.

Vancouver has its faults, of course. Visitors from the Prairies say that it is a nice place, but it is too bad the mountains spoil the view. They also complain that they built the cliffs too close to the roads. Behind the Tweed Curtain, in Victoria, you can't see the retired wheat farmers for the lawn bowling clubs. (They like the flat surfaces.)

If Vancouver has a philosophy, it is that life is not so important as lifestyle. Since there is no alternative to birth and death, the only solution is to smell the flowers on the way through. While the economy supposedly flounders and the nation goes bankrupt, some ninety miles north of Vancouver is Whistler Mountain, the conspicuous consumption capital of the land. At Whistler, money oozes out of the ground, it soars in architectural shapes, it slides down the slopes, money crawls out of the microwaves, money comes on four-wheeled drives and blasts out of the stereos, money sticks to the trunks of the trees.

The weekending Vancouver families prance about on their cowboy heels, adding to the Gross National Product. They zip down the mountain, technicolor streaks against the snow, guardians of our fiscal integrity, selflessly keeping the dollar afloat. Without Whistler, the nation's coffers would choke up and rust.

The genius bringing about this salvation of the Canadian currency comes, appropriately enough, with the mating of Hollywood and the Taxpayer. The newest aspect of the Whistler opulence — development of a whole new mountain, Blackcomb — is a joint operation of Twentieth Century-Fox and Ottawa's Federal Business Development Bank. It is only proper. The illusion of the film world melded with the illusion of fiscal responsibility.

Twentieth Century-Fox's Aspen Ski Corp., which has made that Colorado resort the sex, drugs and rock 'n' roll centre of the universe, has been given a fifty-year lease by the B.C. government to work its hedonistic magic with Blackcomb along with its partner, the feds' bank. It is a marriage made in snow heaven.

Whistler sits in the valley of five lakes — Alpha, Nita, Alta, Green and Lost — two of them connected by the aptly named River of Golden Dreams. It is the river of condominium dreams, one side containing the White Gold Estates, the

197

other side the modest ski chalets of Alpine Meadows, awash in bidets and Gucci-embroidered Jacuzzis.

The new Whistler Village, set on fifty-eight acres between Whistler and Blackcomb, rises splendiferously like a Flash Gordon version of a Bavarian ski town. Some $350 million has been invested so far. There are soaring turrets, clock towers, flying buttresses, steeply banked roofs, tons of stone and copper and angled glass. At night, it looms out of the valley darkness, lights gleaming, like some giant battleship come aground. The Trapp family would freak out. It is Sun Valley updated to the 1980s, the railway barons of the past who built ski resorts replaced by John Q. Public and the men from movie financing who wear tinted shades and forty dollars' worth of haircut.

Arnold Palmer designed the golf course. In condo-world, there is Tantalus. Windwhistle. Brandywine Park Lodge. Wedgeview Centre. The Arthur Erickson-designed Hearthstone. Saunas and whirlpools, hot-tubs and cold champagne. The deli in Whistler Village features Romanoff caviar, canned kumquats and chocolate-covered grasshoppers. The bag lunch packed for skiers is a special gourmet repast: roughing it in the wilderness. The covered parking for condo guests reaches three floors underground.

Whistler is a monster of a mountain. To reach it requires a spectacular, twisting cliffside sprint along one of the B.C. fiords, as beautiful as the Amalfi Drive south of Naples, and then a portage through a canyon that resembles the face of the moon.

The mountain intimidates. One ski run is ten miles long. Thirteen-year-olds rocket by, every one of them wearing a thousand dollars worth of designer pastels. The two hundred dollar moulded plastic boots resemble a piece of modern sculpture stolen from an art gallery. Whistler is named after the marmots that live in the upper region of the mountain. The marmots cower at the colours and shield their eyes. A helicopter whisks jaded skiers to the glacier above. Pierre Trudeau makes his annual pilgrimage and often stays at the condo of his Vancouver dentist. He appreciates the mountain and likes his dentist but doesn't comprehend B.C. anymore than he did his bride who came from here.

Spiffiest of all are the skiers from Tokyo; entire families, tape decks strapped to their chests, earphones injecting John Lennon into their heads, boogie down the mountain. It is the fad of the high-speed skier, enclosed in his own cocoon of sound, with Beethoven or the Grateful Dead, as he sails through the powder snow wrapped in stereo, oblivious to all around, oblivious to the cares of the world, the prototype Vancouverite.

The ultimate in the sybaritic life — and what sums up Vancouver — is the newest fashionable restaurant, L'Orangerie, cunningly stationed within a shanked punt of the new domed stadium that will open in 1983 — if the eighteen-dollar-an-hour construction workers can get in off their yachts, after time off for strikes, in time to finish it. One of the owners, Peter Brown, is a former stock market bad boy who has now reformed. A fortyish millionaire, he is the new chairman of the Vancouver Stock Exchange and likes to order Dom Perignon by the bushel for his friends until the table is awash, rather resembling the plastic tops in beer parlours where they have noon-hour strippers on stage.

The feature of L'Orangerie, copied from an old Paris restaurant, is a sliding glass roof that extends and withdraws at the touch of a finger of a waiter who keeps his eyes peeled for clouds. One usually can go through six changes of season before the brandy arrives.

16
Fifth Digression

The Pretenders

Blue-eyed exile in Winston's . . .
Macdonald was willin' but PET rolled back
the stone . . . Mulroney, the candidate
from Whimsy . . . a tiny, perfect run up the middle . . .
Joe Maybe

The weeds are full of potential successors to Pierre Elliott Reincarnation. The closets echo with their pants of excitement. The curtains rustle as they fidget impatiently, not wanting to disturb the master, who is notoriously stiletto-shy. They await his nod, pawing in the dirt.

John Turner: The Duke of Windsor of Canadian politics, on his own Elba in the left corner banquette in Winston's, the Toronto restaurant that serves, in Peter Newman's phrase, as "the day-care centre for the Establishment." When he was a small child in Ottawa, his mother bought him a dog and he went out on the daily route that Mackenzie King took with his dog. They met. His path was set, foreordained, as boy, youth and man acquiring credentials that can only be topped with the prime ministership. Trudeau doesn't like him because (a) he believes Turner to be not a Liberal at all but a Conservative born accidentally into a Liberal family (true); (b) he suspects Turner fomented gossip about Trudeau's personal life. It is thought that Trudeau will do anything to prevent Turner from taking over, ruining Canada if necessary. He may succeed. Turner pulled back last time when private polls showed he wasn't a sure thing. He has a lot to give up, in the family and pecuniary sense, but he's more in demand this time, the country being in worse shape. Abstinence makes the heart grow fonder.

Don Macdonald: Left with a slight smear of egg on his face last time, after displaying his willingness, when Trudeau rolled back the stone. Would be the choice of party regulars — if there weren't such a thing as popularity polls. Has less hair than Bobby (Jungle Transplant) Hull. Business community likes him. Has thrown careful bread on the water by floating his cautious economic views in the *Globe and Mail*'s Report on Business, the Koran of Bay Street. Would immediately restore the clout of Toronto to the cabinet table. A tough operator, though somewhat mellowed from the Commons days when as Grit House leader he was known as "Thumper" and customarily stepped on the fingers of any Tories hanging from their windowsills. As a careful loyalist to Trudeau, he is still second choice in the public mind to Turner, who has not been. Perhaps there's a lesson there.

Jean Chrétien: Still slightly soiled by his previous stint in finance. He knows he must run this time, since sneaking up behind him in soft loafers is House leader Yvon Pinard, who looks as if he could be, and perhaps should be, on the cover of *Paris Match.* His main handicap is that he is seen as a good, lively Number Two but not quite with the heft for the big job. It would be almost impossible to overcome the determination of Southern Ontario and Western Canada not to have another Francophone following Trudeau. There is practically no one who dislikes Chrétien, but his organizational abilities are suspect. He lives on his nerves and his nerves may be giving out — waiting for the boss to leave.

David Crombie: How much does Joe Clark fear him? Plenty. Is unassailable in key Toronto riding of Rosedale. Preparing quietly for an assault if Clark falters, while letting Brian Mulroney act as the heat-seeking missile. He would like to do, in fact, what Clark did in 1976: sneak up the middle as Mr. Nice Guy while more volatile adversaries take the flak from the flanks. Is an uncommonly adept communicator, which is why Clark has kept him shunted to the sidelines in Tory duties in the Commons.

Brian Mulroney: The jaw that walks like a man may have shot his bolt with his too-publicized national speaking tour that was designed to raise Tory funds. In fact it raised Mulroney's over-weening profile a trifle too high just at a time when MacEachenomics was sending Joe Was into the stratosphere. The Liberal swan dive hurt Mulroney as much as it helped the long-suffering Clark. The Candidate from Whimsy, who wants to start at the top, is not forgiven by large dollops of the party for his reluctance to run a risk. He will not run in a byelection unless he is certain he can win. Politics does not allow that luxury. A man of enormous charm and platform ability, he in fact is trying a remarkable gamble. He is testing whether the Canadian parliamentary system can accommodate an American idea: picking leaders occasionally from the outside who are not actively involved in a formal political role. Mulroney is resentful that, although he has worked in the party as long as Clark (since they were both seventeen) he is regarded as a newcomer. Can he pull off his gamble? Not while MacTrudeau sends the Tories soaring in the polls with their present tenacious leader. It says something about the present bizarre state of Ottawa politics that the three people who most want to become prime minister — Turner, Macdonald and Mulroney — refuse to be a part of the Ottawa scene. The difference is that Turner and Macdonald are seen to have put their families through the gruelling apprenticeship once and are supposedly allowed to rest on the oars of their corporate directorships while in the weeds waiting for the departure of the man who, as someone said of Horace Greeley, fancies himself a self-made man who's in love with his creator.

Paul Hellyer: The Harold Stassen of Canadian politics. A sure-fire entry. The old joke used to be that Hellyer, after bombing as a candidate at both the 1968 Liberal Convention and the 1976 Conservative convention for the same reason — a disastrous leadership speech that he kept secret from his advisors — was headed for the Arctic to teach lemmings how to swim. In fact, he has a good enough sense of humour to mock himself, in his church choir voice, in the skits at the Parliamentary Press Gallery annual dinner now that he is a fairly dull newspaper columnist. Trudeau, from the front row, looks at Hellyer with some puzzlement. Why would a man once seeking the top job in the land mock himself on stage? Hellyer does it because, like practically all politicians, he is a ham. It is why Joe Clark is not a good politician: he does not have the confidence to be a ham in public. Robert Stanfield was appalled at the prospect. William Lyon Mackenzie succeeded because he was his own self-parody.

I digress.

Iona Campagnolo: the one chance for some excitement in the Liberal leadership race. Has the face of an Inca goddess. Would be the Grit equivalent of Rosemary Brown at the NDP Winnipeg convention that chose Ed Broadbent — with no real chance of winning but frightening the whey out of the male contenders. The feminist factor is actually infiltrating the Grit grimace. She is almost as gray as John Turner and even better looking. Liberal men don't trust her ambition and her desire to play the outsider while keeping the umbilical cord slightly attached to the Ottawa Mothership. The constricted Tories of Britain elected, to their surprise, a woman. Would The Bachelor Party be frightened at the contemplation of a woman as a real leadership threat? You betcha.

John Crosbie: a millionaire from one of the four families that own all Newfoundland, a gold medallist at two universities, he discovered early on that his shyness was inhibiting his political ambitions. The solution? Public speaking lessons. Now he knocks them dead while on his feet, but the shyness remains, rolling his eyes upward when asked a question, as a reporter put it, as if contemplating the insides of his eyelids. The rollicking barroom style, laying about him with pun and insult with great gusto, is like a man swinging a broomstick in a crowded Volkswagen van. Probably the best platform performer, all fake outrage, in either party. Unfortunately, his comic gifts and the demands for him to appear as an entertainer at fund-raisers have stereotyped him a bit. The smartest man in a political party is seldom the leader. The ill-confident Clark, who doesn't like rivals with strong personalities, achieved his aim in purposely shifting the ex-finance minister from the much-publicized finance critic post to the shadowland of external affairs critic. He has disappeared from your screen. Some of the boys around Clark play hardball. It is difficult to build a leadership base from "this poor bald rock," as Joey Smallwood calls it.

Bill Davis: He can read. He can especially read Gallup Polls that push the Conservatives, even under Joe Clark, forward when Pierre MacEachen and Allan Trudeau fall behind. So Bill Davis has announced he will stay at Queen's Park, where he has represented Brampton for twenty-four years and where he plans to surpass the twenty-seven years established by former NDP leader Donald MacDonald. Queen's Park always did regard itself as superior to Ottawa.

Peter Lougheed: Is insulted at the suggestion he must go to Ottawa to prove himself. Regards his role in Alberta as the national stage. Is sincere in his desire for a more peaceful private life. Does not regard Ottawa, run by the mandarinate, as reality. He is not a factor in any Conservative search for a new national leader.

Gerald Regan: The former Nova Scotia premier, now Minister of Jockdom among the Trudeaucrats, has two funny quirks in his life. The first is his tennis serve, which starts behind his left ear and emerges from somewhere. The second is his belief that he will be in the leadership race. The serve is only slightly funnier.

Michael Wilson: The tall Tory, a former securities executive, looks like a nonsmoking Randolph Scott and is so straight he would help Boy Scouts across the street. Regards politics as serious business and wouldn't recognize a giggle in a carload. A Clark loyalist up to now, he would be in there slogging if a leadership contest opened.

Edward Schreyer: It has always been the suspicion of this typewriter, which is eternally suspicious, that it has always been the wish of Pierre Trudeau and Edward Schreyer that the one succeed the other. The appointment as governor-general of the first socialist, the first man from the West, the first of ethnic persuasion, was designed by the Grits to win them love, affection and votes in the West. They are now zero for three. However this does not alter the fact that inevitably the Liberals and the NDP are headed for some sort of a merger in Western Canada and social democrat Schreyer can see himself as the link. Underemployed and bored in his current ceremonial role, his problem is how to launder himself so as to be acceptable in active politics again. The only question is: could Lily accept the demotion?

Darcy McKeough: The real white hope dark horse if Clark loses another election. McKeough, big, bluff and hearty, is the John Turner of the Regressive Conservatives: stacked up behind Bill Davis in a holding pattern as Ontario treasurer, he decided to exile himself for a while in business to await a landing spot. As head of Union Gas, he has been collecting corporate directorships like grapes. Big Business loves him. How he would fare in Medicine Hat, with his pinstripes that make him look like a refugee from *Guys and Dolls*, is a moot point.

Eugene Whelan: You think I'm kidding, but he's serious.

Joe Clark: The bland leading the bland. The man who secretly suffers from the disease known as amsirahc — charisma spelled backwards. The man who books a hall that sleeps three hundred. Joe Clark has a strange gift. When he enters a room, people instinctively look up and say, "Who's left?" Joe Was has become Joe Maybe, helped along by pain. His face now shows the signs of a man who has been through fire and has emerged, not safely, but emerged. There are signs of character in it now. Wise political journalist W. A. Wilson has pointed out that while Clark is not strong, he has another quality: resiliency. He has the resiliency of a Brillo pad. Everyone kicks sand in his face, and he returns to the beach for another hotdog. As the Rodney Dangerfield of politics, he can't get no respect. His spine is steeled by the determined, and now stylish, Maureen McTeer. Prematurely frumpish when her husband was elected leader, she was taken to Montreal by Tory girlfriends and pointed in the right directions. She is now, arguably, the best-dressed woman in Canadian politics. Another measure of her will. She hungers for revenge with a white heat. Clark's major problem remains that the talented people one needs to survive in politics will not work for him. His body language gives off negative sparks. His greatest asset is Pierre Trudeau, who may turn him into Joe Gallup.

17
Finale
Trudeau Today
is Nowhere at All

Portrait of Pierre as a non-leader
learning his trade in middle age . . .
Dr. Foth and the PM:
a pleasant little war turned sour . . .
the War Measures Act:
out of the mouth of Spiro Agnew . . .
fade to disillusion

The first time I met Pierre Trudeau was one March Sunday morning in 1968 when we boarded a clumsy Grumman Goose in Vancouver to skip over the Gulf Islands and land in Victoria harbour in front of the Empress Hotel. I was impressed, I see by the back copies, by his "lynx face with high cheekbones and slightly gopher teeth."

Carrying his battered briefcase that contained his change of shirt, he was just one step removed from the international boy vagabond who had never really stuck at any one pursuit — or had to.

A small reception at the Empress, before popeyed matrons and the right sort of Victoria lawyers, was part of his soundings tour to determine if there really was enough national support to push him into the April leadership race.

In the Empress suite, the new hotshot leadership possibility is shaking hands and having tea with twittering party delegates. The press is excluded. But a reporter, hiding behind a teacup, remains unmolested against the wall.

Trudeau moves to the mantle, beneath an immense ornate painting of an obscure English battle. He rests one foot against the hearth, beckons the women in the room to sit at his feet and begins to talk, softly, amusingly, supremely confident, toying with a sandwich. It is the Trudeau of Montreal society, entertaining a few guests at a Saturday soiree.

The women are enraptured, their teacups frozen in their hands. It is easy to see why he prefers small groups. It is easy to see why he masters TV. The charm has an operative range of fifty feet.

After the Goose got us back to Vancouver late that afternoon, there was an excited young girl with tight reddish curls, even then magnetic in her attractiveness, pushing her way through the front row of a crowd that was waiting for the ballroom doors to open in the Hotel Vancouver for yet another reception. When Trudeau appeared, she gave him a quick kiss on the cheek and asked if he "remembered" her from their first meeting in Tahiti. Margaret Sinclair was nineteen.

Over the fourteen years since, there has been the usual cat-and-mouse relationship always endemic to the politician-journalist connection. Reporters and politicians in fact exist in a symbiosis much like prison guards and inmates: in their own peculiar way they are more closely connected to each other than either group is to society at large. They share common interests — and fascinations.

In 1972, your scribbler did a long interview with Prime Minister Trudeau in a hastily requisitioned bedroom in the Fraser Arms Motel in Vancouver — raucous haunt of the University of B.C. beer drinkers — that had a meter on the wall with a message: "This bed is equipped with a massaging unit which quickly carries you off to tingling relaxation and ease. Magic fingers. 25¢ for 15 minutes. Home adaptor unit available."

The Fraser Arms seemed a rather unusual setting to interview a prime minister. It was chosen, one presumed, because it was in the riding of Vancouver South, where Trudeau's former aide Gordon Gibson was attempting to get elected as a Liberal MP, and this exercise was deemed to help. (It didn't. Gibson was defeated, before moving across the water to North Vancouver and trying twice, unsuccessfully, from there. He is now back in the neighbourhood.)

Ignoring the meter, I reminded the prime minister that he took the job almost on a dare, almost as a joke — as he had said at the time — that the press was playing on the country. How had four years of power affected Pierre Trudeau?

212

He grew quite animated at analyzing himself.

"I never imagined myself as a leader. I was always a loner — even during the *Cité Libre* days. That's why I had to have Pelletier as a coeditor — to hold the thing together. I wasn't the type."

He said he had always liked individual sports, "not team sports. Climbing, hiking, canoeing — there were always four-to-six of us in a group. I was never someone who was the leader, though I was forced into it in some circumstances.

How had the job changed him?

"As a professor, as a lawyer, as a writer, I've always been my own man. I called the shots. I made the rules. I can't do this now. This morning I can't just get up and say, 'I'm going to do what I want.' It doesn't work that way."

He explained that when he was "flirting with politics, I could never see myself as part of a team. But when I did go in I realized, 'I'm giving up some of my freedom.'

"I've always been inner-directed. There's the discipline now. More subject to a timetable. At two o'clock every day I have to be in the Commons." For this man, the ordinary disciplines of young manhood didn't come until he was forty-nine.

He talked of the difficulties — meaning the difficulties of a lifetime loner — in running cabinet meetings. "It's more difficult when there's no clear consensus. You have to make sure the team doesn't fall apart."

I got the sense then of someone who had made a career of being a nonleader painfully attempting to grasp the rudimentary tools of running a group of men. It fitted in with the frequent criticism that his cabinet colleagues could never figure out exactly where he stood on issues. Here was a man trying to learn an entirely new trade — while close to the age of fifty-three, two-thirds of his life behind him.

In 1968, Dr. Foth was a cheering fan, climbing off the fence most astonishingly. It's most educational to trip back through the newspaper files and observe my transition in opinion.

5 February 1968 — "Who wants a prime minister who goes around in his bare feet? Exactly! I do."

16 March 1968 — "For anyone who is puzzled by

Trudeau, who is thinking about supporting him — or who thinks he is an evil threat to the country — this collection of his writings [*Federalism and the French Canadians*] provides most of the answers.

"Most of all, there is the clear demonstration of a man who is concerned first with ideas. Whether such an intellectual can master the practical side of the complex world of politics is another matter. Here is a man who has been thinking seriously and pronouncing himself for over a decade on the constitutional and racial problems that have overtaken Canadian politics in the last year or so.

"Trudeau, goes the line, would be a gamble as a prime minister. Of course he's a bit of a gamble. Who wasn't?

"Canada has yet to be run by a leader who has been born in this century. I think that a country that produced Expo should be able to produce as prime minister someone other than a jaded warhorse or a reconverted civil servant. Let's live a little."

2 April 1968 — "I think Pierre Elliott Trudeau would be the best choice from what is available because he holds promise. He would be a good choice to lead a country that holds the same. Trudeau is a pragmatist. He always has been. I would trust him to adjust to the realities once he was saddled with the responsibilities of dealing with a province which, after all, is his homeland."

24 June 1968 — "Since no one has offered the main reason why Pierre Elliott Trudeau will sweep the country tomorrow, it is donated here, free of charge. Eight years ago, Canadians suffered a frustrated longing as they watched Americans elect a president who was young, handsome, rich, intellectual and stylish. He shattered the political taboos. You could feel the Canadian envy. In 1968 Canadians found someone just as attractive. (Canada's choice tomorrow, by the way, will be between two millionaire graduates of Harvard.)

"The Canadian inferiority complex toward Americans has turned into smugness, as we compare what we have with what is now available to Americans. In Oregon last month, James Reston of the *New York Times* queried me intently

214

about this man whose reputation has gone south of the border. U.S. reporters were very interested. For the first time within memory, many Yanks are looking in envy at what we have. We're smug. But if Jack Kennedy had not existed, Pierre Elliott Trudeau would not exist."

16 January 1969 — "The bleat from Mr. P. E. Trudeau concerning the press supposedly interfering with his private romantic life reminds me of Frank Sinatra. Both have achieved fantastic success — in Mr. Sinatra's case, in show biz; in Mr. Trudeau's case, a variation of show biz: politics — exactly because both have received so much publicity concerning their free-swinging, independent ways. Now that they are in power, *they* want to determine which is good publicity and which is bad publicity.

"The point is that Trudeau simply isn't much interested in the press. He won the newspapers over so easily with his casual charm and unorthodox manner last spring, it's natural — human nature being what it is — that he now spurns the panting throng."

26 May 1970 — "It's puzzling that a prime minister of Canada can have this attitude. This attitude, I mean, that he can still determine by his edict what will be printed in the papers and what won't be. That he, in fact, will do the deciding what is 'news' and what isn't.

"There was the sadly familiar story out of Australia last week, Mr. Trudeau and his aides 'furious' that a Sydney paper had front-paged a picture of the prime minister, clad in a brightly-patterned open-neck shirt and beads, dancing snugly in the Taboo Nightclub with an attractive television girl called Bobo.

"Does he really think that photographers would look bliss-fully the other way if an Australian prime minister visited a Vancouver nightclub wearing beads? The fact that Mr. Trudeau is capable of kissing girls in New Zealand and dancing in Sydney is one of the reasons this country flocked to this intriguing man. But his hypocritical view on the reporting of these activities reveals an autocratic streak that is not very attractive."

15 October 1970 — "Yes, indeed things have been peril-

ous these last few days. But try a little test. Take those tough words of Pierre Elliott Trudeau of yesterday on reduction of civil liberties and put them in the mouth of Spiro Agnew. Would you notice any difference?"

4 November 1970 — "The sad fact of the Trudeau government, charged with saving Quebec from itself, is that it is not telling us the truth. Anything less than the whole truth is not the truth.

"We hear, day upon day, hedging hints from minister upon minister that 'if we only knew the truth' we would understand. As each day passes, the suspicion grows — and is supported by talkative cabinet ministers — that the War Measures Act was invoked for political reasons rather than fears of an insurrection.

"We are told to trust the government. But the government, supported by an overwhelming majority of Canadians who have backed Ottawa's action on faith, does not trust us enough to spell out the unpleasant truth."

13 May 1971 — "Mr. Trudeau, drifting along on the swell of his own ego, has been increasingly reluctant to face the grubby minions of the press in full conflict. In fact, he has held fewer press conferences in the past eon than did that reluctant tiger Lester Pearson, never exactly a Georgie Jessel before the mike."

14 October 1971 — "A young reporter for the dying *Toronto Telegram* did a piece the other day on the changing mores of Our Leader, one Pierre Easily Trendeau. Our Leader, recounted the reporter, had displayed an interesting switch in tactics lately, in line with his changing status in the opinion polls.

"Our Leader, it was detailed, had taken to actually talking to backbench Liberal MPs. Our Leader, it was said, was getting absolutely chummy with the ink-stained wretches who chase him down the halls. The other day, in a chat with some minions, he playfully punched one of them in the stomach and nudged another in jest.

"So yesterday, emerging from Question Period, Our Leader was beset by the same group of reporters in quest of the usual daily information. In mock imitation of the article, he playfully

216

punched one of the two girl reporters, both under 30, in the throng of a dozen males.

"No, he didn't want to comment on that. Don't you have anything to say, the retreating figure was asked? Yes, he playfully replied as he went through the door, and the phrase rang out from Our Leader's lips, 'Fuck off.' Most instructional, it is, to do the social round these days."

And so on. For a long time there was a good adversarial atmosphere, a mutual needling. Deadpan, Trudeau would step on my foot as he emerged from press conferences. Once, when my newspaper editorial board hosted him at lunch, he entered the dining area, shook hands solemnly with all present, and then punched me in the chest. It was a pleasant little war, both sides enjoying it.

But over the years, as the needling sharpened into something stronger, there was a change. While the PM claims never to read the newspapers, he is in fact supplied with daily selected press clippings by aide Joyce Fairbairn. As Richard Gwyn pointed out in his brilliant book on Trudeau, *The Northern Magus*, the reason he pretends not to know what is in the press is that he can't stand being criticized.

I was writing during the first Trudeau decade for the *Vancouver Sun*, which at that time had the second-highest circulation in Canada and was the largest paper in Western Canada. As the Liberals sank lower in fortunes in our end of the world, it seemed logical that the party would like to use its prize communicator to explain its no-doubt-misunderstood message. Requests for interviews became Byzantine struggles, translated through scores of nervous aides and often killed near the top by such as Senator Perrault, who had the puzzling philosophy that those who criticized should be punished by being sent to Coventry.

Eventually, as the manipulators (and the nervous ones) around Trudeau purposely shut off access to anyone who might be rough on him, the relationship simply hardened into war. Between 1976 and 1978, they loosed their tiger to fifty-three sessions on radio and television, fifteen encounters with the foreign press — and only thirteen to Canadian print journalists. More foreigners were allowed to interview Canada's prime minister than Canadian reporters — an accurate gauge of the distaste felt by the PMO for the increasingly critical national press.

During his winning 1980 election campaign, Trudeau gave a total of twelve interviews (as opposed to ten while losing in 1979). Just three of them were to the despised pencil press.

(I was granted another long interview in his Centre Block office some years after the Fraser Arms episode. The relationship went downhill from there.)

Perhaps it is time to dispel the standard misconception that still rests among some portions of the public, namely that the press "elected" Trudeau in 1968. The press did no such thing (oh, that we had the power). The press is simply a radar system, a DEW-line, as McLuhan said, out there ahead of the public, paid to sniff the wind.

The press, along with its junior cousins in the electronic jockey field, was out in front of the public on the 1968 Trudeau because it could detect an incipient public interest. In the same way that the press soured on Trudeau before the public did — the voter disillusion subsequently followed. That's what radar is for.

(The sins of the press come when it isn't far *enough* in front of the public — as in the Parti Québécois sweep in Quebec, or the Olds-Didsbury byelection.)

At the close of the Economic Summit in Venice in the summer of 1980, Trudeau held a press conference for Canadian reporters and I asked him, since he would be host at the 1981 summit in Ottawa, if that would fulfill his goals and would he then proceed to his retirement as he had earlier indicated.

He replied that "there are stranger things in politics than are written in the stars and, as to my retirement, one can only speculate and — in your case — hope."

The next night, in Rome, after Trudeau had taken his son Justin to see the Pope, he was to have a small midnight dinner at the penthouse apartment of Roloff Beny, the Medicine Hat photographer who had become an international name for his posh coffee table books, including the unfortunately timed tribute to the Shah of Iran.

I was invited along by Suzanne Perry, a Trudeau press secretary. It was a magnificent summer night. Beny's sumptuous three-floor apartment as exquisitely decorated as could be imagined, overlooked from its rooftop garden the sluggish Tiber below with the lights of Rome beyond. We sat under the potted trees as several ladies prepared scrambled eggs filled with smoked salmon, and when Trudeau realized your shy agent was present, said, "Oh, God, *Fotheringham*. I can't go *anywhere* but you're there."

One thing about Fotheringham he admired, he went on to the assembled guests, "is that you make enemies so easily. You remind me in that way of Cyrano de Bergerac. If you had any culture, you'd know" — and he launched into a passage of Cyrano in French.

"Oh, Mr. Prime Minister," I said, "I couldn't possibly have any culture. I'm from Western Canada."

Trudeau left shortly after. That encounter two years ago was really the last. After that, the Trudeaucrats hived into their bunker mentality vis-à-vis Western Canada. Your scribbler, I suppose, now reflects the general Western attitude: the government and its leader have given up on half the country. It's simply a matter of waiting them out.

Most all Canadians underestimate what a freak Pierre Trudeau is — a freak in the sense of how long he has been around. He is the longest-reigning leader in the western democracies. The United States has gone through five presidents since Trudeau came to power: Lyndon Johnson, Richard Nixon, Gerald Ford, Jimmy Carter and now Ronnie Reagan.

The Brits have gone through five prime ministerial terms: Harold Wilson, Edward Heath, Wilson again, James Callaghan and now Maggie Thatcher. When Trudeau was elected, Chancellor Kiesinger was running West Germany, followed by Willy Brandt and Helmut Schmidt. France has moved from

Couve de Murville to Gisgard d'Estaing to Mitterand in the same time span. Italy has circulated a Rubik's cube of names, which are as forgettable as those Prince Edward Island premiers.

If Trudeau wishes to beat the longevity record of French-Canadian prime ministers, as he has hinted, he would stay until April 1984, to beat the term of Sir Wilfrid Laurier. The record for a democratically elected leader is Prime Minister Tage Erlander of Sweden, in power for 22 years, 357 days.

Trudeau has now been in power himself longer than all the Progressive Conservative leaders since World War I. He has been more successful, in terms of political longevity, than Messrs. Meighen, Bennett, Manion, Bracken, Drew, Diefenbaker, Stanfield and Clark put together.

The problem, from our point of view — me and thee voter — is that as his quite underestimated seniority advances, his real interest in the country at large diminishes, rather than increases. He has a shrinking vision of Canada, dominated by his constitutional obsession, but is incapable of venturing much beyond that. He is a brilliant, but limited, man.

During the Depression, doomed Prime Minister R. B. Bennett wore a top hat throughout. Pierre Trudeau, in the worst unemployment and economic conditions since the Depression, wears a fresh rose in his lapel morning, noon and evening. There is a link.

Only history, of course, will assess Trudeau, but there have been preliminary attempts. Richard Gwyn concluded that he was a magician, and a dull, stolid country of the cold north was fascinated by such a quicksilver character. My friend George Radwanski, in his more sympathetic treatment, has been jibed a trifle too much for his assessment that Trudeau is not so much a failure as "unfulfilled." (The Argentine forces were not defeated in the Falklands; they were unfulfilled.)

This corner suspects that the judgment of time will applaud Trudeau for what is currently regarded as his greatest failure: Quebec. The criticism is that the man who went to Ottawa to save Quebec has had to watch while a separatist government was voted into power. In fact, his brave and stubborn determination to impose official bilingualism on an ostensibly bilingual country (with a streak of prejudice still running underground) probably stalled the progress of the independantistes.

If he had not arrested the smug superiority of English-Canada and alerted it to its responsibilities, Quebec would have, one suggests, embraced a separatist-bent party even sooner than it did. Trudeau couldn't halt the progress of cultural forces in his own province, but he did bend them a bit and bought some time.

His faults lie in another direction. Relentless in his determination when it comes to things that interest him, he descends into lassitude and indifference when it comes to things that don't. It's why he has allowed the Liberal party to die in the four Western provinces where the future growth of population is headed.

There is the strange impulse that moved him, on one of his rare forays into Regina, to twit the locals about their "hysteria" over the gas and oil slump caused by his National Energy Policy. The same impulse, almost a political death wish, impelled him to lecture a Liberal gathering in Banff this spring on the Alberta delegates' unseemly obsession with oil and gas, a stunning insight that taken to its uttermost, might dissuade Maritimers from being too concerned with fish or British Columbians from being too worried about their failing lumber markets. It is a lordly attitude, ethereal, infuriating, contemptuous.

The disappointment in him is devastating. In 1967, Peter Newman wrote in the *Toronto Star*: "Unlike the unreconstructed political dinosaurs of the Liberal party who still occupy most of the positions of power, Trudeau is an agent of ferment, a critic of Canadian society, questioning its collected conventional wisdom . . . [He makes] our national future appear very bright indeed." In 1982 Newman as editor of *Maclean's* called for his resignation. The *Globe and Mail* does the same, saying of a man heading a majority government that still has a three-year mandate ahead of it: "He cannot solve our problems because he is the problem."

221

Especially in my part of the country. Because he does not understand the West, he has given up on it — and, in the process, vitiated his party.

Last year, Vancouver's Simon Fraser University (Margaret's alma mater, a school that Trudeau has never visited in his fourteen years of power) had a two-day conference honouring F. R. Scott, the legendary Montreal socialist, poet and constitutional lawyer. Trudeau attended a reception in a downtown hotel for the great man, who was eighty-one, as old as the century. It might have been useful for him to recall what Frank Scott wrote in *The Dance is One*, a 1973 collection of his poems:

> By moving West
> I learned how to go East . . .
> Wanting to go somewhere
> I started in the other direction
> At last I know where I am
> I am nowhere at all.

Pierre Trudeau is nowhere at all. Despite his 1971 resolve, he never mastered being a team man and so gave up on it. He didn't try to keep a team together and the players are now on the outside, waiting for his removal.

In the end, the vigorous sixty-three-year-old on the trampoline proved to be a *lazy* leader. He gave evidence, in the final judgment, to support the worst charge against him in the beginning: he is a dilettante.

Acknowledgements

This book would not have been written without the inspiration, encouragement and support of Anna Porter, a publisher whose determination is exceeded only by her sense of humour. Both were sorely tested in this project. It owes much to the hand-holding of Don Obe, the skillful steering of Paula Goepfert and the sharp eyes of Judith Brooks. Their tolerance is greatly appreciated.

I am grateful to my employer, Southam News, and to *Maclean's*, under whose banner I have gathered the material over the years that provided the evidence for this diatribe. My acknowledgments are due Allan Hustak's *Lougheed* and the late David Lewis' *Corporate Welfare Bums*.

I must pay tribute to the unique contributions made by Alexander Ross, Jack Batten, the tape of Supertramp and Ballantine's. Without them, this page would not exist.

Allan Fotheringham was born in Hearne, Saskatchewan on August 31, 1932. "The town," he writes, "was so small we couldn't afford a village idiot; everyone had to take turns." He went to a one-room schoolhouse (containing 12 grades), where he spent most of his time outdoors, snaring gophers with a length of binder twine. "This," he says, "proved educational for later use in political journalism."

Eventually he moved to B.C. ("which improved the IQ of both provinces") with his family. He went to Chilliwack High School, where he wrote a column for the school paper, and the University of British Columbia, where, naturally, he wrote a column for the *Ubyssey*. He joined the sports department of the Vancouver *Sun* after graduation, leaving three years later to travel and write in Britain, Europe and Russia. He returned to the *Sun* as a travel writer, then spent a sabbatical year at the University of Toronto on a Southam Fellowship. For the next four years, he sharpened his outrage as a member of the *Sun*'s editorial board. He was given a column in 1968 and for 11 years used his notoriously cutting style to expose every bit of sham, cant and outright double dealing he could find. But, his work had another significance, as Ron Haggart, a fine columnist himself, now turned TV producer, has pointed out: "Fotheringham brought Vancouver a wider view of the nation than the narrow B.C. outlook. It was a major contribution; it had a real effect."

It also brought him national attention. In 1975, while still at the *Sun*, he began his reign of the back page of *Maclean's*, a bi-monthly, then weekly forum that sent him on his way to becoming Canada's most controversial columnist. In 1979, he left the *Sun* to write a national column for the FP News Service in Ottawa; he switched to the Southam chain just before FP News folded in 1980. His column appears in the 15 Southam papers and is syndicated to five others. He continues to be the best-read feature in *Maclean's*.

These days, he practises a kind of shuttle journalism, living two weeks of the month in Vancouver ("the hot tub and water bed concession of the world") and two in Ottawa ("Ennui-on-the-Rideau," where "minds are stuffed with bafflegab and mouths filled with persiflage — and vice versa"). He has been called — quite correctly — "the greatest cobweb blower and guff-remover in Canadian journalism."